W9-BJL-002
Exorcist
Kazue Kato

Blue Exorcist

Contents 27

CAST OF CHARACTERS

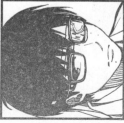

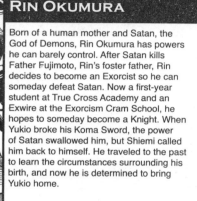

THE KNIGHTS OF THE TRUE CROSS

RIN OKUMURA

Born of a human mother and Satan, the God of Demons, Rin Okumura has powers he can barely control. After Satan kills Father Fujimoto, Rin's foster father, Rin decides to become an Exorcist so he can someday defeat Satan. Now a first-year student at True Cross Academy and an Exwire at the Exorcism Cram School, he hopes to someday become a Knight. When Yukio broke his Koma Sword, the power of Satan swallowed him, but Shiemi called him back to himself. He traveled to the past to learn the circumstances surrounding his birth, and now he is determined to bring Yukio home.

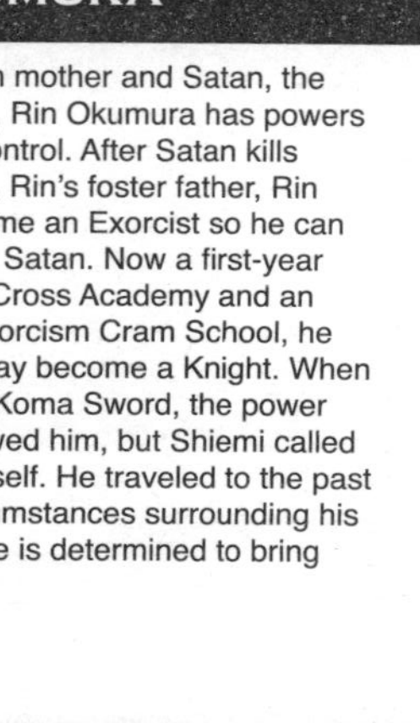

YUKIO OKUMURA

Rin's brother. He's a genius who is the youngest student ever to become an instructor at the Exorcism Cram School. He left the Knights of the True Cross and went over to the Illuminati, but that was so he could gain information about Satan possessing his left eye.

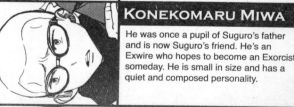

SHIEMI MORIYAMA

Daughter of the owner of Futsumaya, an Exorcist supply shop. She possesses the ability to become a Tamer and can summon a baby Greenman named Nee. After quitting the Exorcism Cram School, she went to a garden called El inside Vatican headquarters, where she began training.

RYUJI SUGURO

Heir to the venerable Buddhist sect known as Myodha in Kyoto. He wants to achieve the titles of Dragoon and Aria. He is Lightning's apprentice and they were conducting an investigation together.

KONEKOMARU MIWA

He was once a pupil of Suguro's father and is now Suguro's friend. He's an Exwire who hopes to become an Exorcist someday. He is small in size and has a quiet and composed personality.

IZUMO KAMIKI

An Exwire with the blood of shrine maidens. She has the ability to become a Tamer and can summon two white foxes. The Illuminati had taken her captive, but with help from Rin and the others, she escaped and settled her grudge against the insane professor Gedoin.

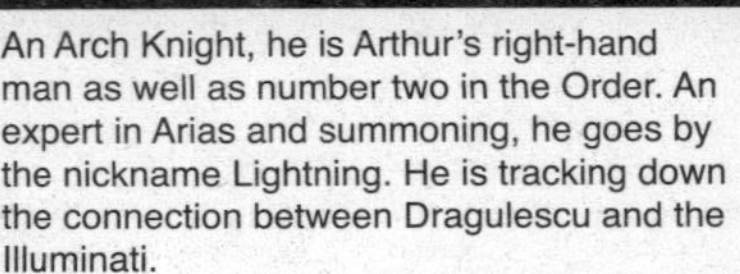

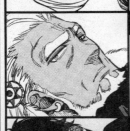

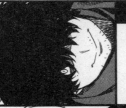

Lewin Light

An Arch Knight, he is Arthur's right-hand man as well as number two in the Order. An expert in Arias and summoning, he goes by the nickname Lightning. He is tracking down the connection between Dragulescu and the Illuminati.

Lucy Yang

An Arch Knight from the China Branch.

Osceola Redarm

An Arch Knight from the Mexico Branch.

Igor Neuhaus

A Senior Exorcist First Class who holds the titles of Tamer, Doctor, and Aria. Under orders from Mephisto, he was researching enhanced anti-demon compounds.

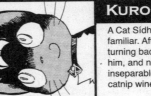

Mephisto Pheles

President of True Cross Academy and head of the Exorcism Cram School. He was Father Fujimoto's friend, and now he is Rin and Yukio's guardian. He's a high-ranking demon known as Samael, King of Time. He promised to raise Rin as a vessel for possession by Satan.

Kuro

A Cat Sídhe who was once Shiro's familiar. After Shiro's death, he began turning back into a demon. Rin saved him, and now the two are practically inseparable. His favorite drink is the catnip wine Shiro used to make.

THE ILLUMINATI

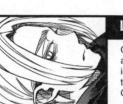

LUCIFER

Commander-in-chief of the Illuminati. Known as the King of Light, he is the highest power in Gehenna aside from Satan. He is plotting to bring Satan back and unite Assiah and Gehenna.

EGYN

One of the Baal and known as the King of Water. Assistant director of the airborne research laboratory on *Dominus Liminis*.

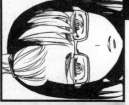

HOMARE TODO

Leader of Phosphorus, an organization of guards directly under Lucifer's command. She is Saburota Todo's daughter and Shima's superior officer, and holds a rank of Adeptus Minor or higher.

DRAC DRAGULESCU

A former Arch Knight. As a researcher at Section 13, he was leading research into cloning for Satan and Lucifer. He continued his research later and has been in secret communication with the Illuminati.

RENZO SHIMA

Once a pupil of Suguro's father and now Suguro's friend. Currently, he is a double agent providing information to both the Illuminati and the Knights of the True Cross.

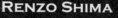

SATAN

Rin and Yukio's father. He is connected to and rules over almost all demons. He has occupied Yukio's left eye in order to spy on Assiah.

The Story So Far

Both human and demon blood runs through Rin Okumura's veins. In an argument with his foster father, Father Fujimoto, Rin learns that Satan is his true father. Satan suddenly appears and tries to drag Rin down to Gehenna because Rin has inherited his power. Father Fujimoto fights to defend Rin, but dies in the process. Rin decides to become an Exorcist so he can someday defeat Satan and begins studying at the Exorcism Cram School under the instruction of his twin brother Yukio, who is already an Exorcist.

Rin and the others succeed in defeating the Impure King, awakened by the former Exorcist, Todo. Meanwhile, Yukio fights Todo, and as the battle rages, he senses the same flame in his own eyes as his brother.

Later, mysterious events begin occurring around the globe orchestrated by a secret society known as the Illuminati. Finally, the Japanese government publicly recognizes the existence of demons.

In order to learn about Satan inhabiting his left eye and the secrets surrounding his birth, Yukio tells Rin goodbye and goes to join the Illuminati. Traveling through the past, Rin learns how Shiro and Yuri felt about himself and his brother. Then, in an effort to bring Yukio back, Rin once again appears before him.

Yukio tries to make Rin kill him before Satan can use him, but Rin decides to use force and starts throwing punches. However, Satan's protection blocks Rin's attacks. Running out of options, Rin unleashes his flame. He stops just shy of finishing off Yukio, restrains his power, and burns Satan out from inside Yukio, thereby successfully separating them. However...

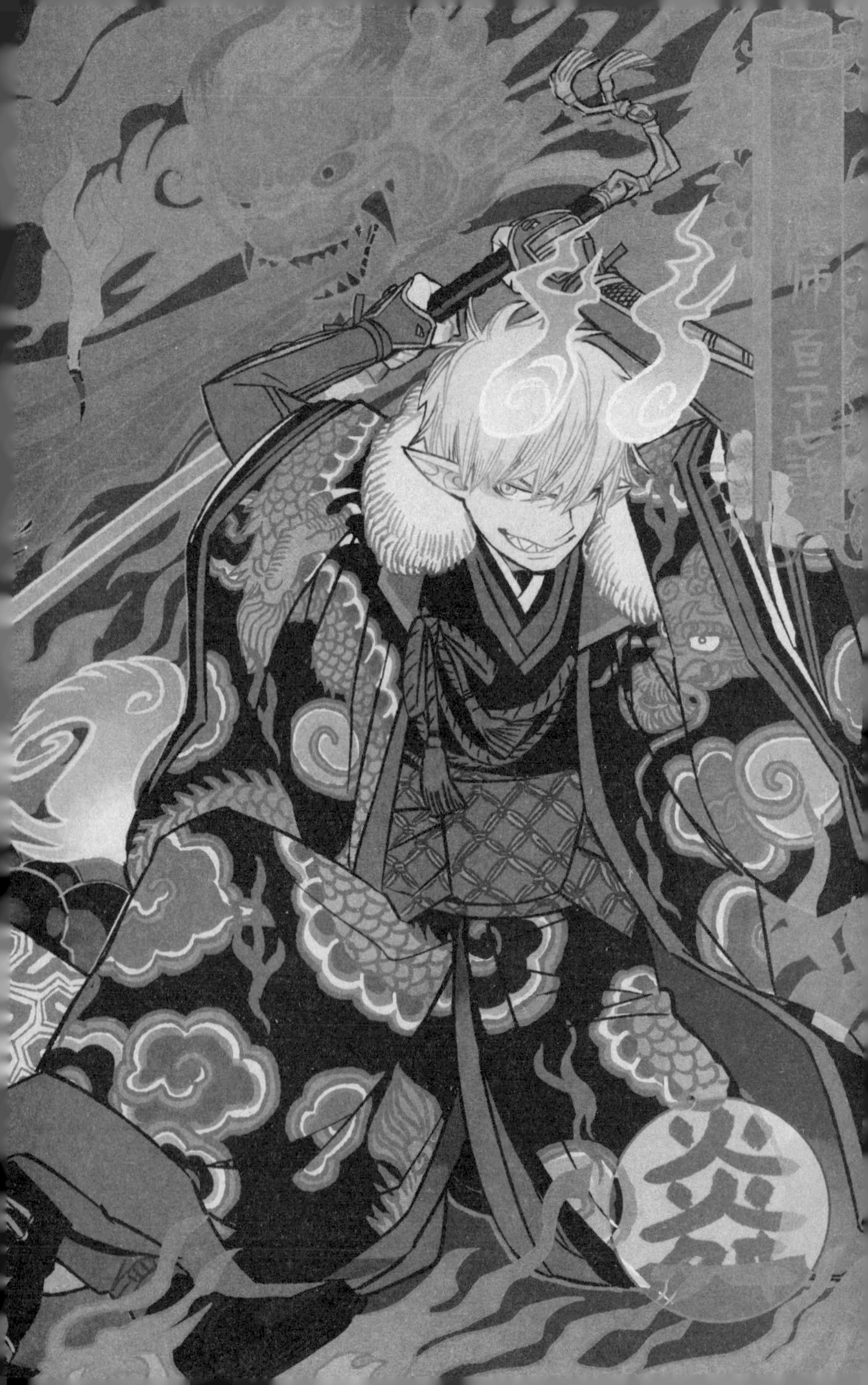
炎

Chapter 126:
Of One Cloth—Sundered

CAUTION
The following chapter starts a bit back in time.
It's not a mistake.
It's on purpose.

RMM
RMM
RMM
BF
BF
BF
BF
RMM
RMM
RM M

RMM
BWOOM
RMM
RMM

THOOOM
RMM
RMM
RMM

ZSH
ZSH
ZSH

ZSH
ZSH

WHOA!!
...
...HOLY SH-!
WHUP WHUP
WHUP
WHUP
WHUP
GWOOOOOO

I'LL FIND A PLACE TO LAND!
HURRY!!

BWF
BWF
BF
BF

BWOOSH

THUMP
ZSHHH

WHAM
KTNK
SHWP
CHING

HEY...

YES?

DO YOU REALLY THINK YOU'VE WON...
...JUST BECAUSE YOU GOT THAT JUNKY SWORD BACK?

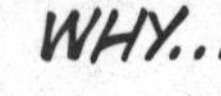
WHY...

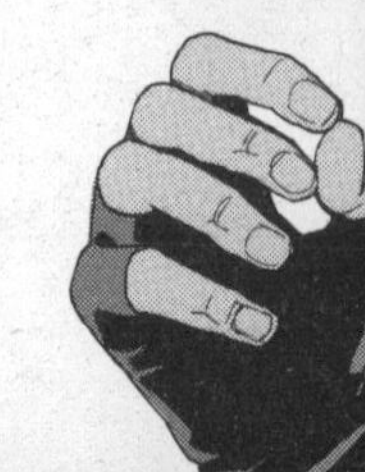

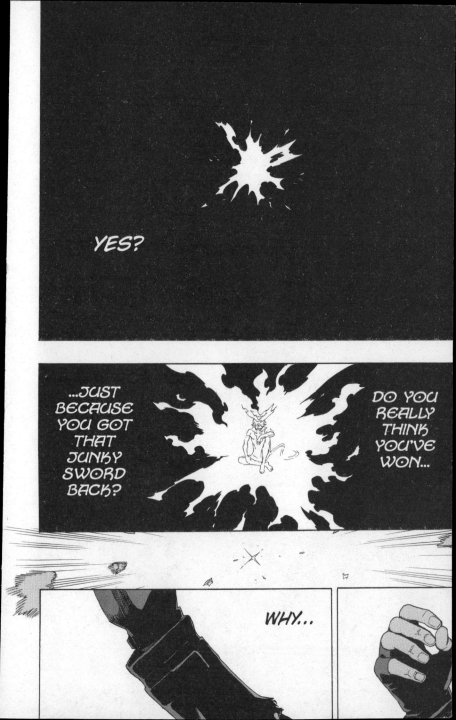

...WAS I ALWAYS...
...SO SCARED OF YOU?
FWAP

FOOF
WHAT...
...DID YOU...
...JUST SAY?
I AM YOU!
YOU CAN'T GET RID OF ME...
...OR RUN AWAY FROM ME!!
FO
OM
ZZZT
ZZZ
I KNOW THAT.

SO...
...I'M GONNA TAME YOU.

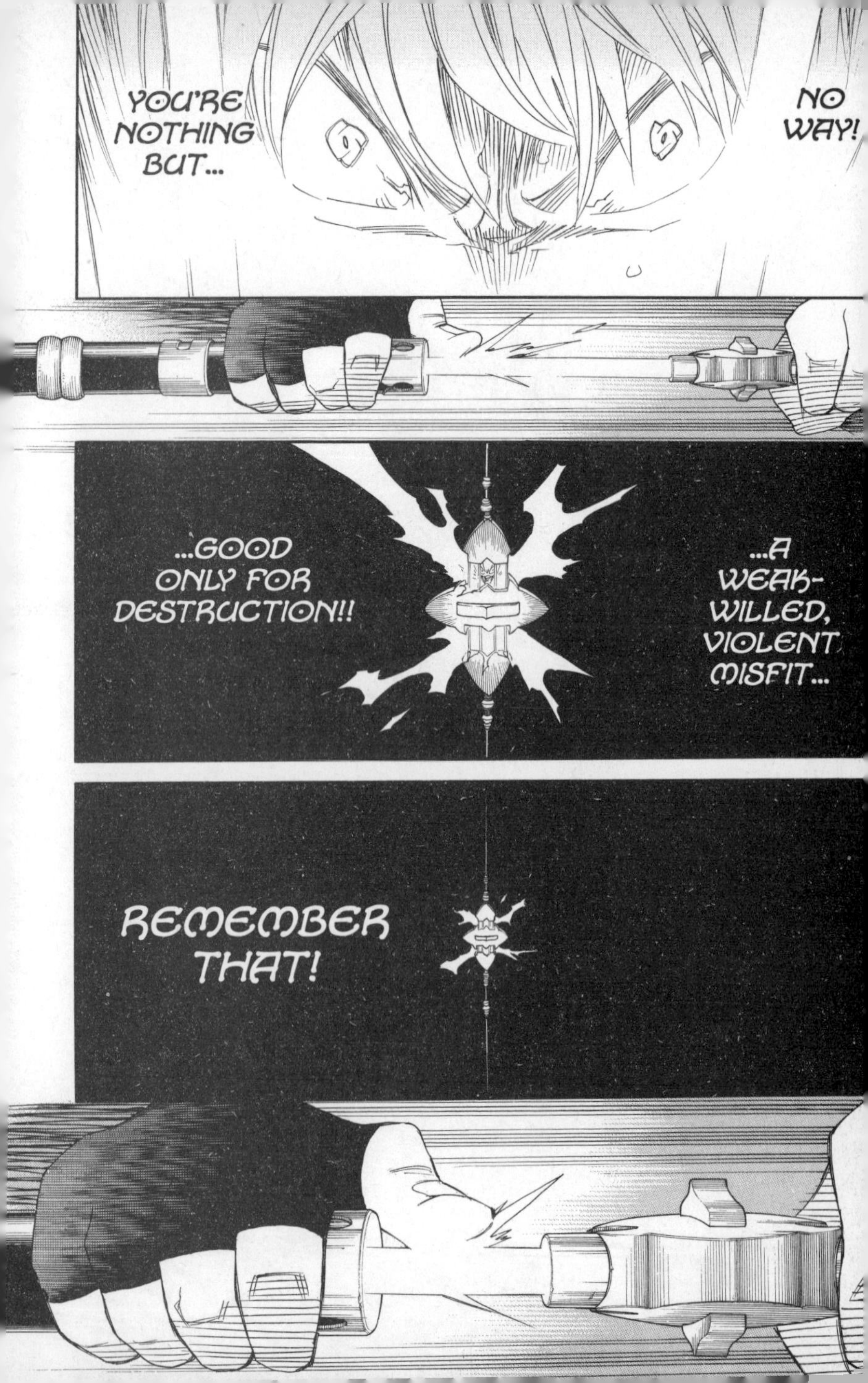
NO WAY!
YOU'RE NOTHING BUT...
...A WEAK-WILLED, VIOLENT MISFIT...
...GOOD ONLY FOR DESTRUCTION!!
REMEMBER THAT!

SHNK
FWSH

YEAH, I *WILL* REMEMBER THAT.

IT'S A SEA OF FLAMES DOWN THERE.
FO
OO
OO
HUH?!
HWOOO
MAYBE THIS'LL SLOW DOWN...
...LUCIFER'S PLANS A LITTLE.
...BUT...
IT'S TOO SOON TO KNOW IF THAT'S TRUE...
...HAVE YOU NOTICED THAT YOUR HAIR IS BLACK AGAIN?

SERIOUSLY?
I DON'T KNOW WHAT HAPPENED, BUT...
VREEE
...I'VE FIRED NINE SHOTS WITH THIS PROTOTYPE. YET THE BATTERY IS STILL TWO-THIRDS CHARGED.
VREEEE
WHAT DO YOU THINK WILL HAPPEN...
...IF I PACK THAT WHOLE CHARGE INTO ONE SHOT?
BOOM

TH
WAM
SKIDDD
KRASH
KLATTER
THUD

KRUMBL
KTUNK
JOLT
GET UP. THERE'S NO TIME.

SATAN COULD COME BACK AT ANY MOMENT.
CAN'T YOU DO THIS WITH YOUR MONSTROUS STRENGTH?
...

I FEEL ...
... SORTA WEAK.

I'M GLAD...
...TO HEAR THAT.
KLUNK

??
WHAT DO YOU MEAN?!
WHAM
KRUNK
NOW YOU'RE BASICALLY NORMAL.
KLNK
KLATTER
AND SO AM I UNTIL SATAN RETURNS.
NOW WE CAN HAVE A FAIR FIGHT.
OH, RIGHT...
I KNOW YOU'VE GOT A CHIP ON YOUR SHOULDER, BUT...
...TRY NOT TO LOSE YOUR HEAD, OKAY?
JUST STAY CALM.

I'M GOING TO SET MATTERS STRAIGHT!!
I HAVE **NEVER** BEEN ABLE TO STAY CALM!

EVER SINCE MY EYES CHANGED...
...I'VE WANTED TO *DIE.*
G
I TRIED COMMITTING SUICIDE MANY TIMES.
W
O
BUT NOTHING WORKED.
O
YOU COULDN'T KILL ME EITHER.
NO ONE CAN KILL ME.
HUH?

THAT'S WHY...
...I HAVE TO DO SOMETHING ABOUT IT MYSELF.
BUT YOU WANT TO STOP ME.
SO WE HAVE TO FIGHT.

SUICIDE?!
MANY TIMES ??
W...
WHEN?!
WHAP
WHEN DID THAT START?!
I HAD NO IDEA!

SO WHILE YOU...
...WERE GOING THROUGH ALL THAT...
...I MUST'VE LOOKED SO STUPID!
...!!!
Y...
Y...
...
Y...
YOU...
YOU'RE ALWAYS LIKE THAT!!
OUR CIRCUMSTANCES WERE DIFFERENT...
...SO I NEVER SAID ANYTHING, BUT...
...YOU KEEP DOING THIS!
TAKE YOUR SEATS, PLEASE.
WHAH WHAH WHAH WHAH
SORRY...
IF I'D TOLD YOU, YOU WOULDN'T HAVE REACTED SO CONVINCINGLY...
ENEMY BY FOOLING YOUR ALLIES?!
OKAY, FINE! I FORGIVE YOU!!
YOU REALLY AWESOME
THANK YOU...
IT'S NICE TO MEET YOU
I'VE JUST BEEN TIRED...
...BUT I'M FINE NOW.

YOU ALWAYS LIE!
YOU'RE A LIAR!!

COULD YOU...

...AND YOUR BRAIN HAVE SOLVED ANYTHING?

DAMN YOU!!
WHSH
FWP FWP
WHP
!
WHOK
YOU'VE BEEN LIKE THAT...
WHSH
KCHK
GUH!
...EVER SINCE WE WERE KIDS!
THOK

I COULDN'T TELL ANYONE ABOUT ANYTHING!
!
STAGGER
UNGH ...
WHAM
SO WHAT WAS I SUPPOSED TO DO?!
THMP
HUFF
HUFF
KOFF
BUT...
KRUMBL

BMM
HUH?
...YOU COULD'VE TOLD ME IN SECRET!!
RMM
RMM
RMM
YOU WERE IN TROUBLE...
...AND THERE I WAS LOOKING STUPID!
THU
D
GUH!
HA!
"HEY, BRO, GUESS WHAT?
YOU'RE SATAN'S BASTARD CHILD..."
WH
NGH!
"...SO ALL THE EXORCISTS FEAR AND HATE YOU!"
WHAM
WHUD

WAS I REALLY SUPPOSED TO TELL YOU THAT?!
I KNEW IT...
HE REALLY IS TOUGH!
TMP
BUT... NO!!
SO...
!!

...IS THAT HOW YOU FELT TOO?!
THAT I WAS SCARY ?!
YOU...
...COULD...
...HAVE...

...TOLD ME!!!!

FMP

BAM

WHY ?!

WHY DIDN'T YOU RELY ON ME?!!

GRAB
GRAB
WHP
WHP
?!
GRN
CH
YOU DON'T RELY ON ANYONE EITHER!

SHNP
HAVE YOU EVER RELIED ON ME?!
BLAM

Blue Exorcist Chapter 126: Of One Cloth—Sundered

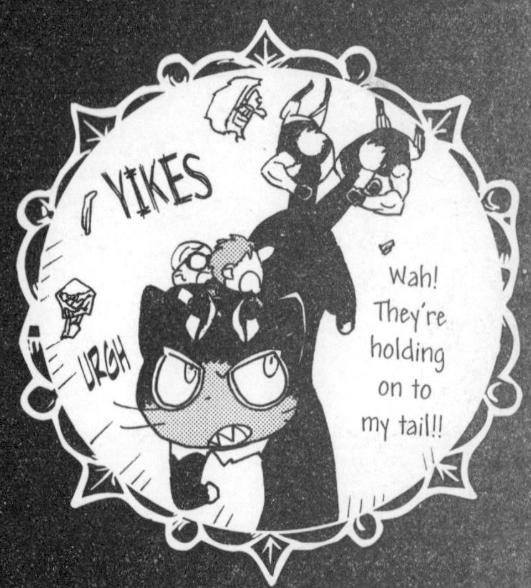

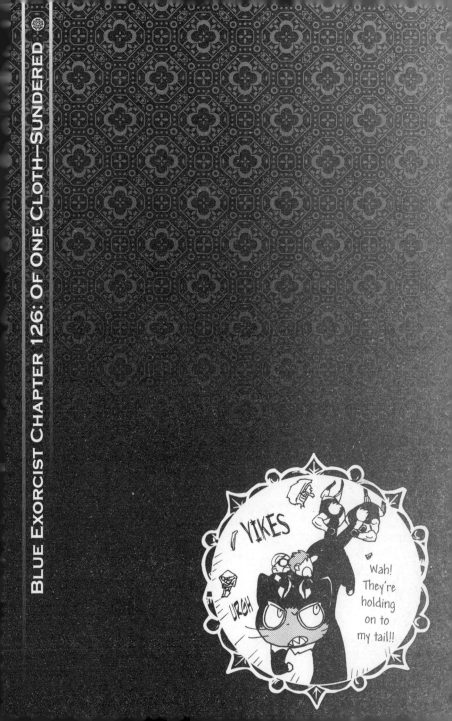

LIKE YOU'RE ONE TO TALK!!
BLAM
BLAM
BLAM
BLAM
CHAPTER 127: OF ONE CLOTH—THAW
SHMP
G...
GAGH!

GRND

YOU'RE THE ONE WHO ALWAYS TRIES TO SHOULDER EVERYTHING YOURSELF...

GUH...

UGH...

GRND

GRND

...EVEN IF IT KILLS YOU!!

IT WOULD BE BETTER IF I'D NEVER BEEN BORN.

SO I SHOULD BE CRITICIZING YOU!!!
OH...
UMMM
...IN THAT CASE...
!
PH
...WE'RE PRETTY SIMILAR!!

SLAM
WE NEVER SHOULD'VE THOUGHT...
...WE WERE TOO DIFFERENT TO UNDERSTAND EACH OTHER!
GRAB

?!!
FWUP
TH
WAM
NO, WE *ARE* DIFFERENT !!
WE'RE OPPOSITES IN EVERY WAY!
WOW! HE'S FAST!
!!

YOU'RE STRONG, SO YOU NEVER RELY ON ANYONE AND TAKE A LOT OF RISKS!!
WHAM
BUT...
WHAM
...I'M WEAK...
!!!
BAM
BAM
BA
...SO I'M UNRELIABLE ...
...AND JUST WANT TO DIE!
WHAM
UNNN...
...NGH!
CLAMP

GAN
WHAT'S WRONG?
GRN
YOU'VE GOT MORE THAN THIS!!
STOP HOLDING BACK!!!!
GRN
HRR...
GRN
GRN
GRN
...RGH!
I'M...
...NOT...
...HOLDING...
...BACK!!

WHAP
KOFF
KOFF
KOFF
?!
STOP PLAYING AROUND.
BRING OUT YOUR DEMON!!
IF YOU DO, YOUR STRENGTH WILL COME BACK!!
HUFF
HUFF

HUFF HUFF

...I ENJOY FIGHTING ON EVEN TERMS.

ISN'T THIS WHAT *YOU* WANTED TOO?

I JUST WANTED TO REMOVE ALL DISTRACTIONS!

WHM
YOU'RE SO CLUELESS!
P
YOUR POWERS GET TAKEN AWAY...
!
THMP
FW
UP
...I PISTOL-WHIP YOU...
TA
TUMP
...AND YOU'RE NOT EVEN MAD?!
BAM

ARE YOU STILL ENJOYING THIS?!

BAM

GUH!

NO...

...THE WAY YUKIO MOVES...
...AND USES HIS BODY...

...SHOWS HOW HARD HE'S WORKED.
EVEN THOUGH HE USED TO BE..

...PHYSICALLY WEAK...
...AND GOT BULLIED...

THOK
...AND WAS A BIG CRY-BABY.
GAH!
THMP
STAGGER
GAG
UGH...
KOFF
KOFF KOFF
HUFF
HUFF
HEH...
HA HA...

SNIFF
YOU KNOW WHAT?
HUFF
HUFF
YOU'RE PRETTY TOUGH.
NO...
...THAT CAN'T BE!
THDM

BWSH
THAT...
WHNK
...CAN'T BE!!
YOU'RE ...
...A LOT STRONGER!
THAT'S WHY...

...I WANTED TO GET STRONGER!

I DIDN'T WANT TO RELY ON ANYONE!
UNN...
... NGH!
I WANTED TO SOLVE EVERYTHING MYSELF!
I WANTED TO BELIEVE I COULD DO THAT...
...LIKE YOU!!

I WAS ALWAYS FRUSTRATED.
AND...
...I HATED MYSELF FOR BEING WEAK AND SMALL.
IT WAS JUVENILE SELF-LOATHING.
AND I COULDN'T STAY LIKE THAT FOREVER.
I UNDERSTAND THAT RATIONALLY...

YUKIO...
...BUT I CAN'T GET PAST IT!!
...I FINALLY...

...
UNDER-
STAND-
YOU!

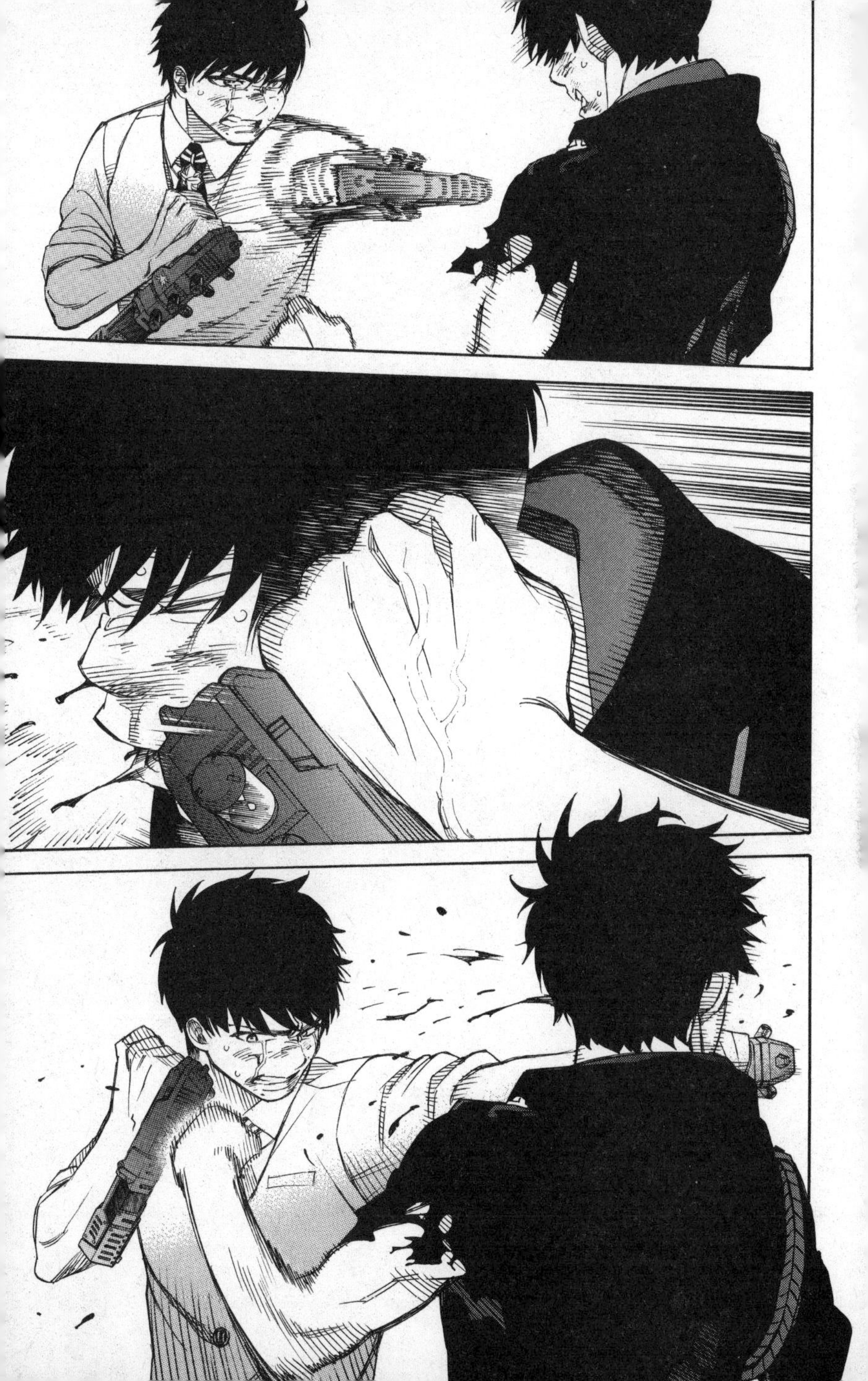

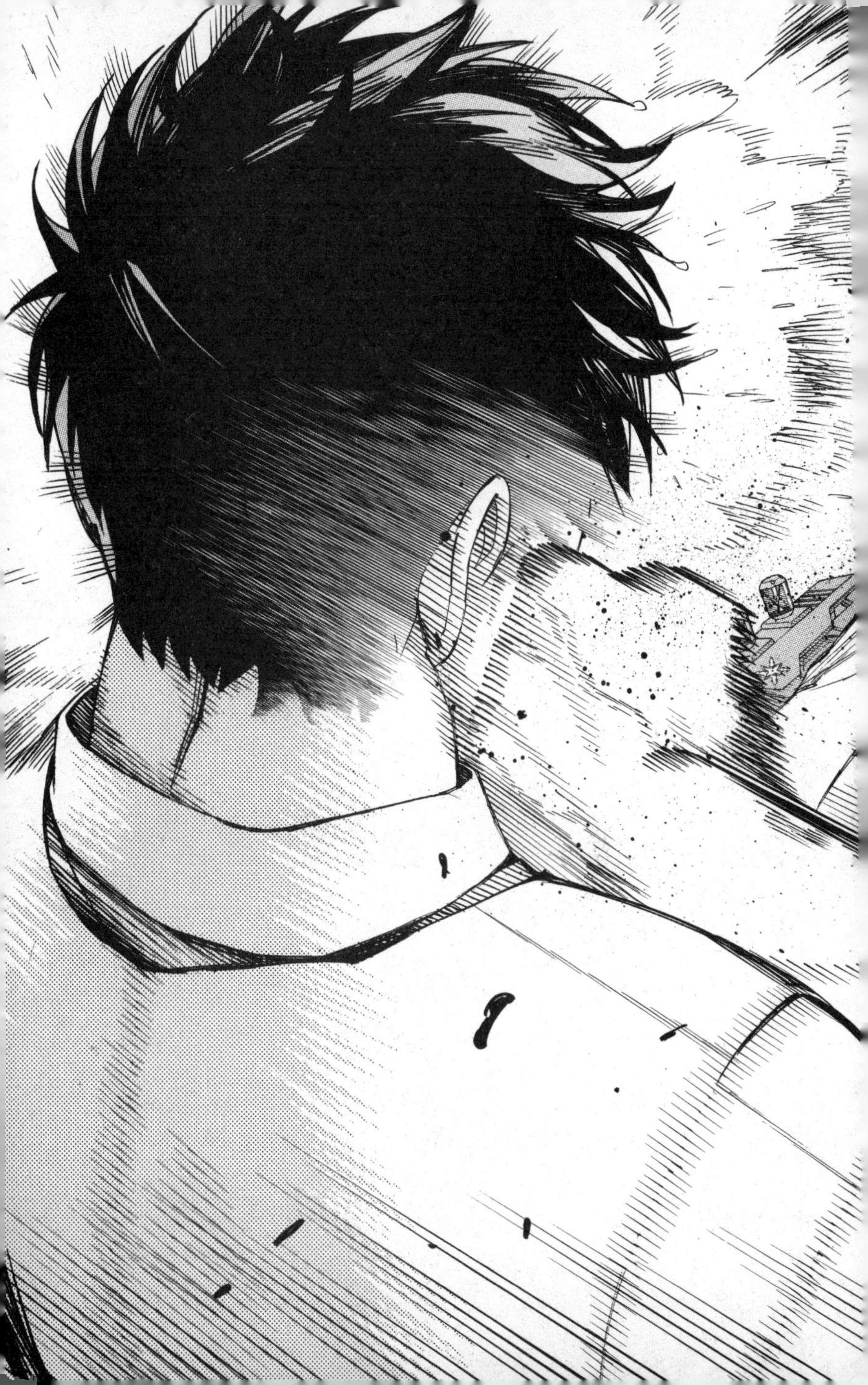

HUFF
HUFF
WHEEZ
HUFF

HUFF
HUFF
I CAN'T STAND IT...

I DIDN'T WANT TO CRY LIKE THIS.
IT'S LIKE...
...WE'RE KIDS AGAIN!
WHAT...
...ARE YOU TALKING ABOUT? LOOK AT ME!
HUFF
HUFF
YOU'RE ALREADY STRONG!
HUFF

MY OBSESSION WITH WORLD CRISES...

...THE ORDER AND FATHER FUJIMOTO...

...AND THE CIRCUMSTANCES OF OUR BIRTH...

IT WAS ALL...

...AN EXCUSE TO HIDE MY ***WEAKNESS***!

DO YOU...
...REALLY THINK...
...I CAN KEEP LIVING LIKE THIS?

YES, THAT'S WHAT I WANT YOU TO DO!

IF I'M STRONG...
...IT'S BECAUSE I HAD YOU!

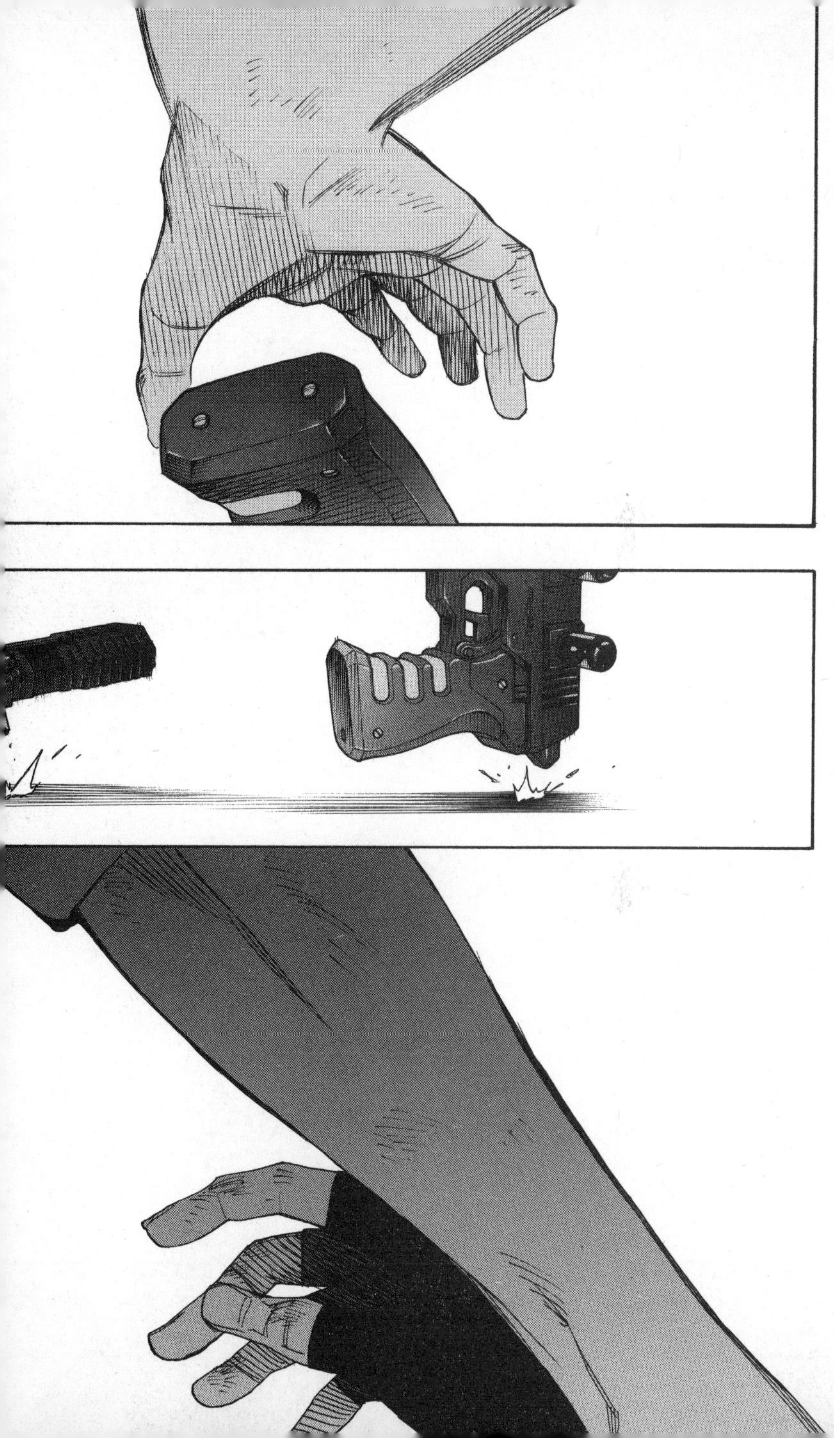

HUFF
HUFF
HUFF
HUFF

...IT'S BECAUSE OF *YOU*!!

Blue Exorcist Chapter 127: Of One Cloth—Thaw

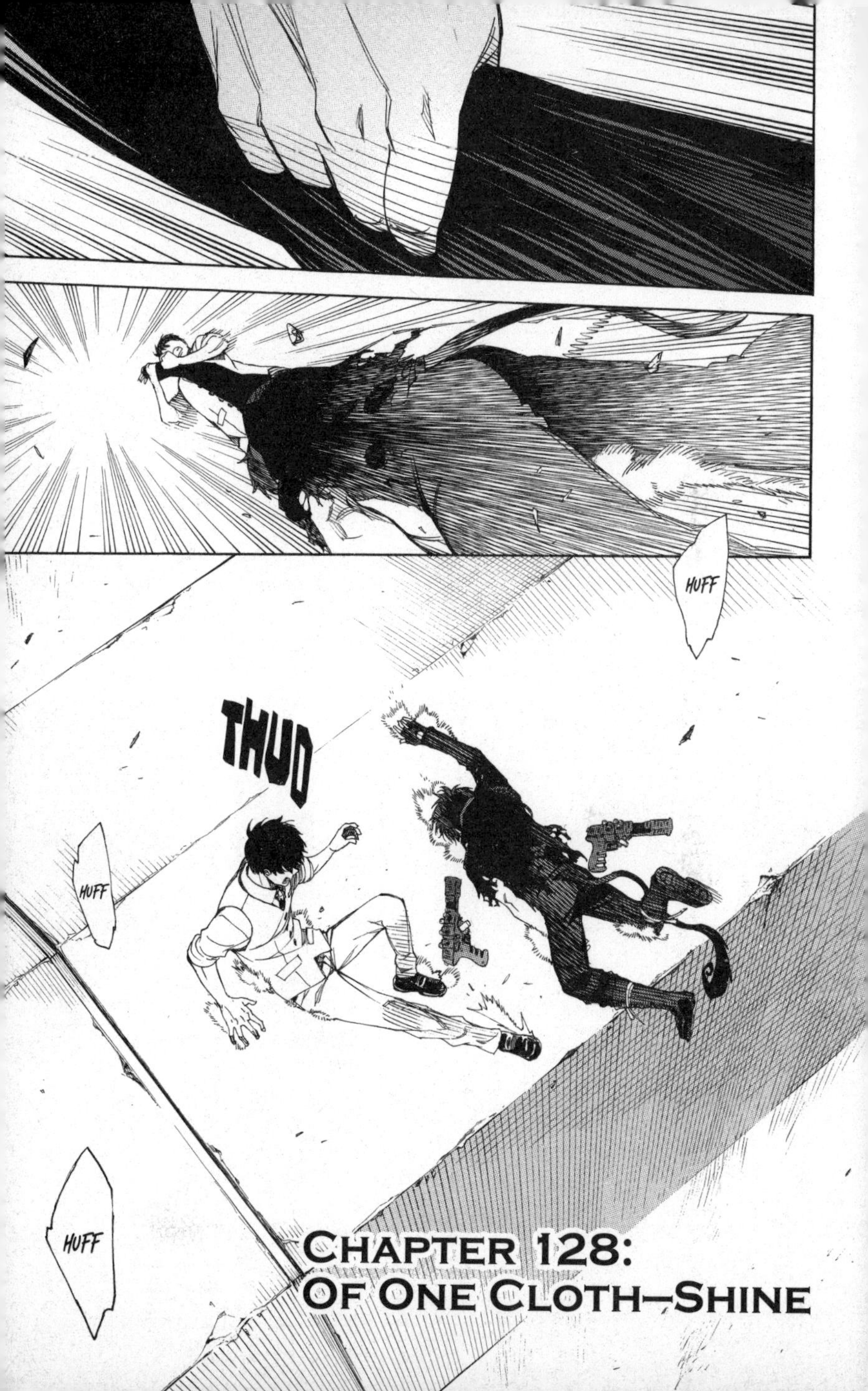
HUFF
THUD
HUFF
HUFF
Chapter 128:
Of One Cloth—Shine

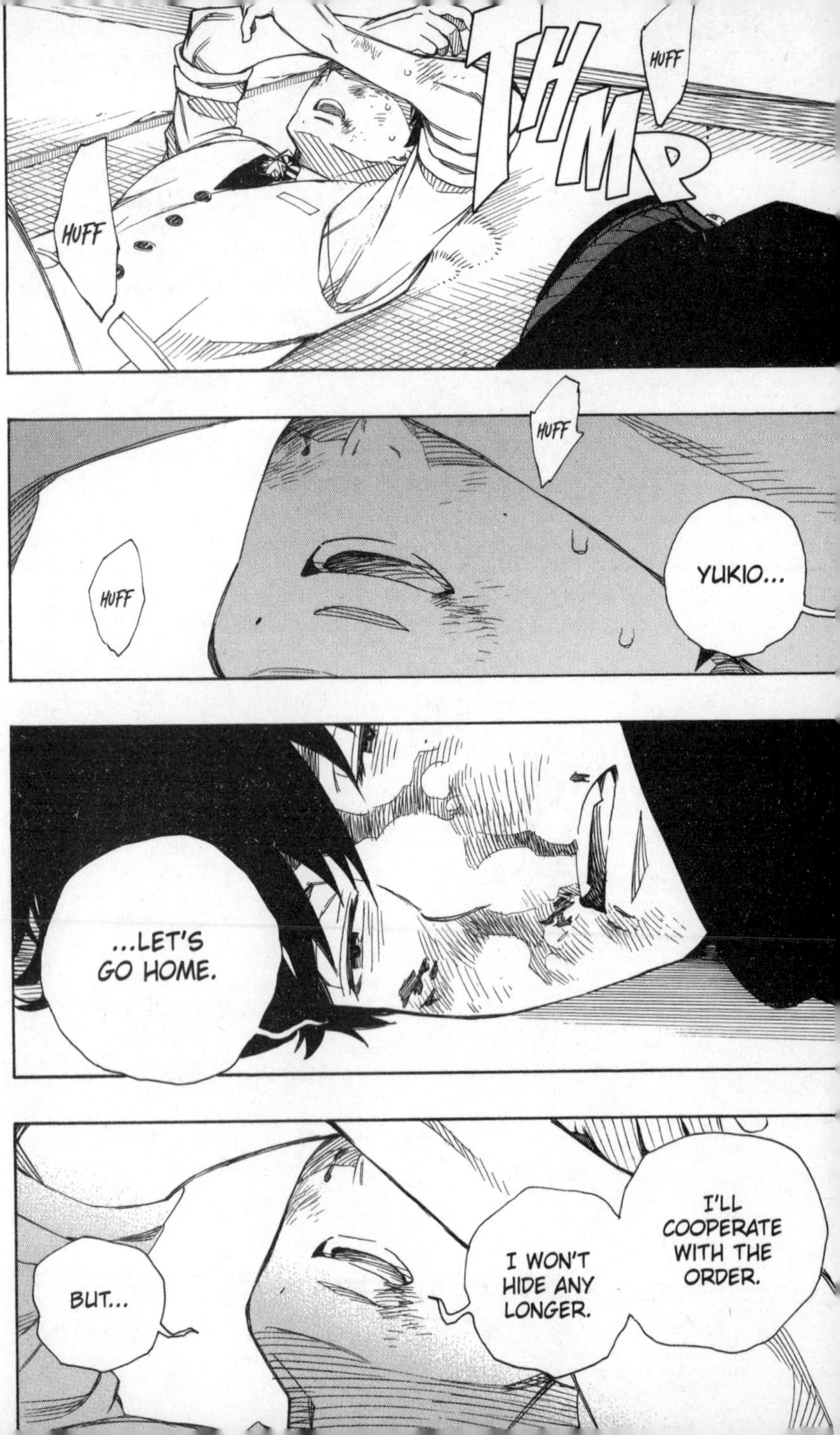

HUFF
THMP
HUFF

HUFF
YUKIO...
HUFF

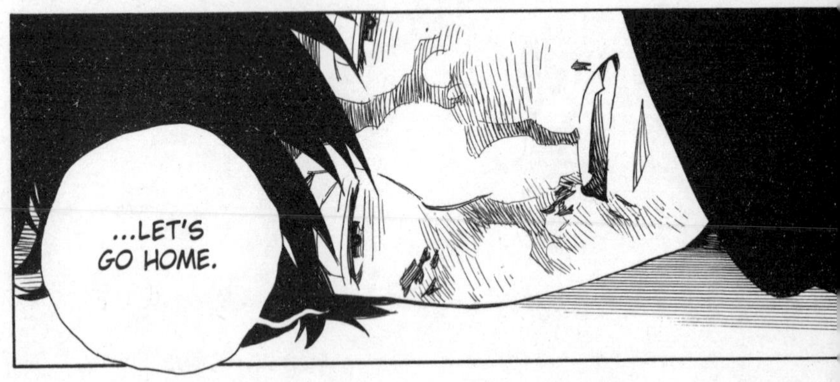

...I CAN'T JUST...
...GO BACK.
I MADE AN UNFORGIVABLE MISTAKE.
WHO SAID...
...IT WAS UNFORGIV-ABLE?

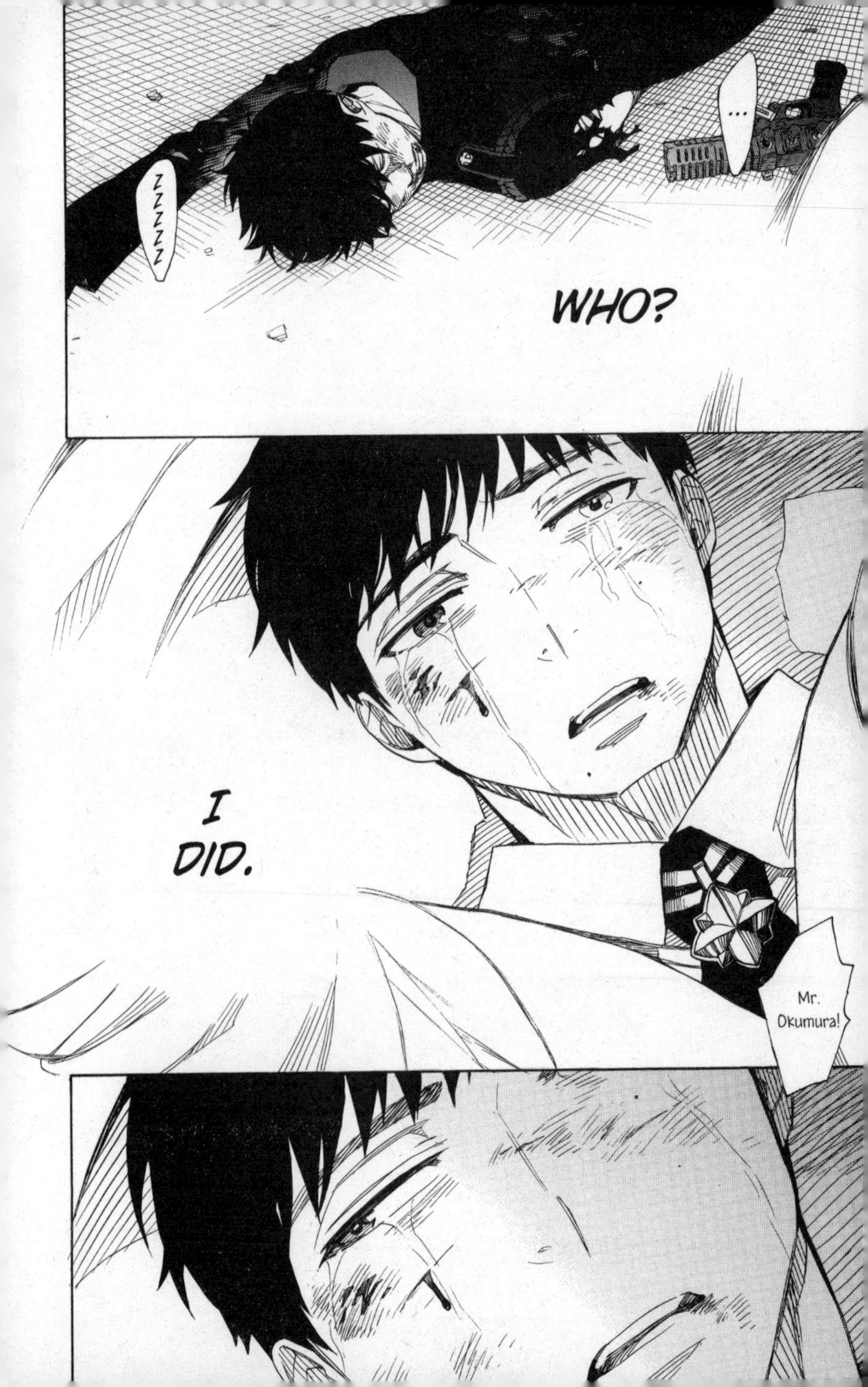
...
ZZZZZ
WHO?
I DID.
Mr. Okumura!

Are y-you all right?

Hey!
Move aside.
Let me see.

HE'S MERELY UNCONSCIOUS.

IT'S NOT SERIOUS.
AND I THINK THIS GUY IS JUST ASLEEP.
OH, GOOD.
AW, MAN... I'VE GOT A TON OF QUESTIONS! CAN I WAKE THEM UP?
Y-YEAH, YOU CAN TRY...

G
W
O
A SMALL CONFRONTATION RESULTED IN IMMENSE DESTRUCTION.
IT'S LIKE SOMETHING FROM MYTH.
OO
HWOO
WHAT DO WE DO NOW?
FIRST, WE HAVE TO FIND LUCIFER AND DRAGULESCU.
AND WE MUST CONFIRM THAT THEIR RESEARCH LIES IN ASHES.

WE NEED MORE PERSONNEL.
AND RESOURCES.
IT'S TOO COLD HERE.
I'LL PUT IN A REQUEST IMMEDIATELY.

WHAT ABOUT SHIMA?
HMF!

HWOO
...
HE HAS YAMANTAKA, SO I BET HE SURVIVED.

ANYWAY, HE CHOSE THIS PATH HIMSELF.
BWOOSH

IZUMOOO! ♡
IT'S ME—SHIMA!
THE ONE YOU'VE ALL BEEN WAITING FOR! ♡
AND ME TOO—KONEKO-MARU!!
THWAM

OH, WOW.
AH, SHIMA. GOOD WORK.
LIGHTNING! WE FOUND SOMETHING!

RMM
RMM
RMM
DOCTOR DRAGULESCU...
RMM

...WHAT WERE YOU TRANSPORTING?

MUTTER
MUTTER
HOW COULD YOU...
...DO THIS ?!
MUTTER
MUTTER
THIS IS TERRIBLE!
MUTTER

I DEDICATED MY LIFE TO THIS RESEARCH!
BUT YOU...
YOU...
...DESTROYED IT!!

SATAN DID ALL THIS BY POSSESSING YUKIO OKUMURA...
...SO IT'S YOUR OWN SIDE'S FAULT.

ARE YOU TELLING ME...
...THAT HE'S *HERE* ?!
HA HA...
HEH...
HEE HEE...

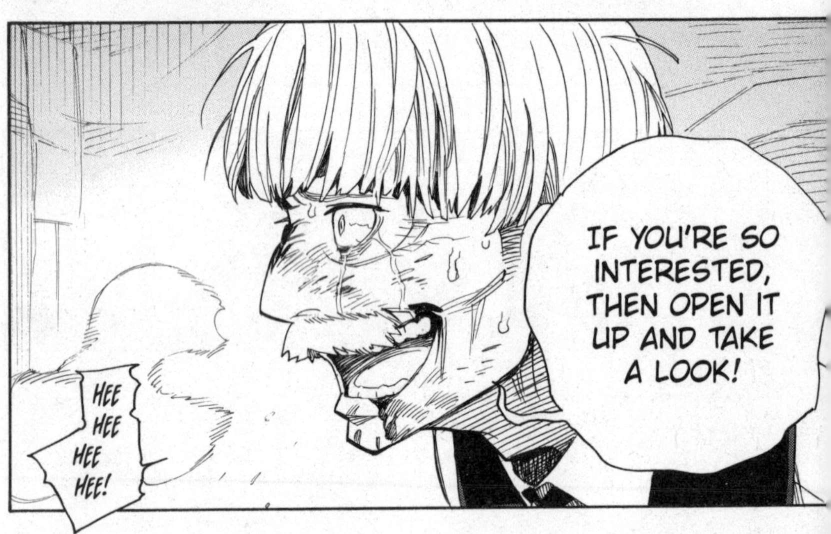
IF YOU'RE SO INTERESTED, THEN OPEN IT UP AND TAKE A LOOK!
HEE HEE HEE HEE!

HE'S GIVING ME THE CREEPS.
YES. WE SHOULDN'T OPEN IT.

TAKE DRAGULESCU INTO CUSTODY...

...AND DON'T LET ANYONE GO NEAR THE STORAGE UNIT.

YES, SIR!!

!

MY INTUITION TELLS ME THIS IS BAD.

AND YOUR INTUITION IS OFTEN CORRECT.

WE'LL TAKE TURNS SEARCHING THROUGHOUT THE NIGHT.

FWUP
OH...
...Y-YUKIO...
...DID YOU GET SOME SLEEP?

TELL ME...
...YUKIO OKUMURA...
...HOW'S YOUR CONDITION?
OKAY...
...SURE.
GLANCE
FWUP
I'M FINE.
I APOLOGIZE FOR CAUSING WORRY DURING THIS EMERGENCY.
I LOST CONTROL OF MYSELF.
AND I'M READY FOR DISCIPLINARY ACTION.
YOU'RE STILL YOUNG...
...AND YOU'RE IN A TRICKY POSITION, SO THE FAULT IS ALSO OURS.
BUT I JOINED THE ORDER OF MY OWN FREE WILL...
...SO YOU HAVE TO—
THAT DOESN'T MATTER NOW.

FIRST, THANK YOU FOR SUMMONING MY FAMILIAR.
POMF
IF YOU HADN'T...
...WE WOULD'VE ARRIVED TOO LATE.

WERE YOU ABLE...
...TO CONFIRM COMPLETION OR DESTRUCTION OF THE ELIXIR?
!!
NO...
...NOT ITS DESTRUC-TION.
SORRY.

OH WELL...
...AT LEAST YOU BOUGHT US SOME TIME.
WE'RE SEARCHING THE CRASH SITE...
...AND FINDING QUITE A LOAD OF GOODIES.

LIKE A BODY FOR SATAN.
WHAT ?!

...
IF THAT'S TRUE...
...THEN I SHOULDN'T BE HERE.
YOU SHOULD KILL ME OR CONFINE ME BENEATH THE VATICAN.
I BELIEVE THE ILLUMINATI WANTS ME...
...TO TELL SATAN IN GEHENNA...
...THE LOCATION OF HIS VESSEL FOR POSSESSION.
IT'S TOO RISKY FOR ME TO BE IN THE SAME PLACE AS THE BODY AND THE ELIXIR!!
CALM DOWN.

EVEN IF WE KILLED YOU OR LOCKED YOU UP...

...WHEREVER YOU WENT WOULD BE A BATTLEFIELD...

GASP

...SO THERE WILL ALWAYS BE A RISK OF SATAN'S RETURN.

I HATE TO WASTE STUFF...

KRIK

...SO I'M RETURNING THESE.

BAM

?!

WE ALSO FOUND SOMETHING LIKE BATTERIES, SO PUT 'EM TO USE.

REST TODAY, AND GET BACK TO WORK TOMORROW.

HUH?

NOW HOLD ON A SECOND!

THINGS CAN'T STAY THE SAME AS BEFORE!

DO SOME-THING ABOUT ME!

DO YOU REALLY WANT TO BE PUNISHED?

GASP

I CAN'T FORGIVE MYSELF...

WHY?

LIKE YOU SAID, THIS IS AN EMERGENCY...

TAK TAK TAK

...SO WE CAN'T WASTE TIME DISCIPLINING YOU.

ACCORDING TO YOUR DOSSIER...

...YOU HAVEN'T TAKEN THE PROMOTION EXAM, BUT YOU HAVE THE SKILLS OF A SENIOR EXORCIST.

SO I *CAN* USE YOU.

I'LL USE EVERYTHING I'VE GOT...

...EVEN ***DEMONS*** AND ***PERPS.***

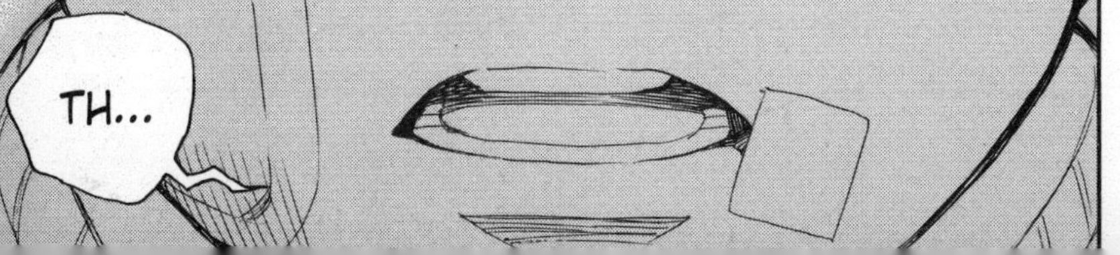

THANK YOU...!!

BOW

...VERY MUCH!
SWIP
FWUP
?
WHY WAS HE SO GRATEFUL?
HEH!
HE DOESN'T WANT ANYONE TO TREAT HIM WITH CAUTION.

INSTEAD, HE PREFERS YOUR COLD RATIONALITY.

REALLY?

BUT REGARDING PLAN B...

...SOMEONE SHOULD BRIEF SIR PHELES.

OH?

I WANTED TO AVOID THAT...

...BUT I GUESS THERE'S NO CHOICE.

PUFF

PUFF

PUFF

WOW! THAT LOOKS DELICIOUS!!

IT'S ALMOST READY.

GO TELL THE OTHERS.

YES, SIR!!

WHOA

YAY

YAY

FWIK
!!
WAP
YUKIO?
WHSH
THIS HOT WATER...
...WILL WARM YOU UP.
KRAK!
KRAK!
KRAK!
HERE, SHIMA.
THANKS.
UGH...
THANKS, BUT I NEED CALORIES.
I'VE BEEN WORKING SO HARD, I NEED TO RECHARGE.
YOU JUST HAVE TO WAIT UNTIL IT'S DONE COOKING.

AH!
OKUMURA! ARE YOU ALL RIGHT?!
SLURRRP
GOOD MORNING, OKUMURA.
MORNIN'!
YOU'RE ALL...
... HERE!
W-W-W...
WAAAH! IT'S BEEN SO LONG!!
I'M SO GLAD YOU'RE ALIVE!!
HUG
?!
YEAH, I SURVIVED.
AH HA HA!
YOU'RE ACTING LIKE IT'S BEEN YEARS.
RIN!
I DID MY BEST TO HELP!
THANKS, KURO!
HOP
RUB

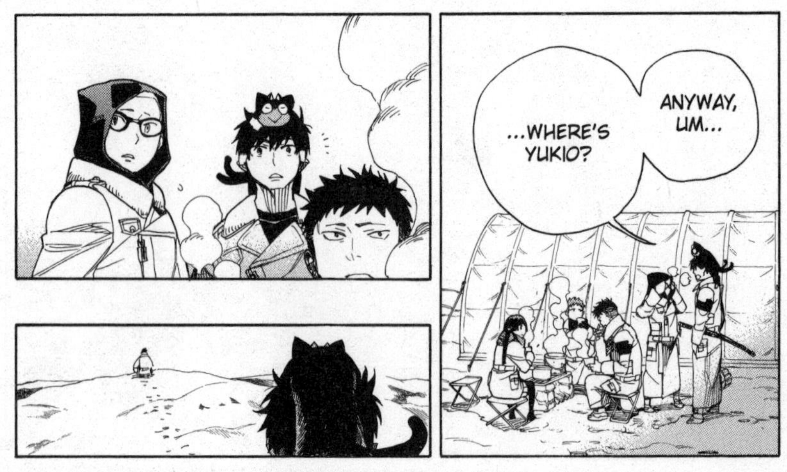
ANYWAY, UM...
...WHERE'S YUKIO?

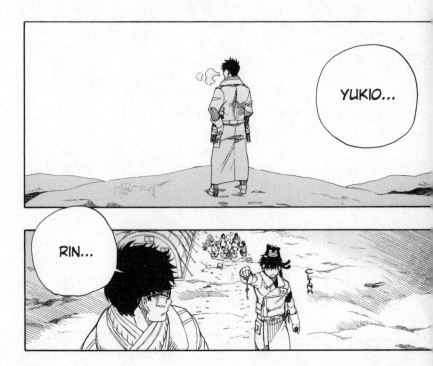

YUKIO...

RIN...

CLINK

LET'S GO INTO THE PAST TOGETHER.

FATHER FUJIMOTO AND MOM...

...MADE MISTAKES TOO.

AND I'VE MADE A THOUSAND MORE MISTAKES THAN YOU.

BUT I DON'T THINK I WILL.

WHY NOT?!

WHY WOULDN'T YOU?!

SERIOUSLY ??!

WAAAAH

I THOUGHT IF I KNEW THE PAST...

...AND DIDN'T RELY ON ANYONE...

...AND BEHAVED CORRECTLY...

...AND BECAME STRONG...

...THAT THE PAIN WOULD GO AWAY. BUT I WAS WRONG.

BUT THAT'S WHAT I WANT TO DO.
SO I WON'T GO.
OH, OKAY...
...I CAN UNDERSTAND THAT.

THEY WERE SUPER COOL!

MOM DIED PROTECTING US...
...AND SHE WANTED US TO GET ALONG.
OH, REALLY?
UH-HUH!
HEEEY

HEEEEY

I GOT US BREAK-FAST!

AWESOME!

LET'S GO. I'M STARVING.

RIN!

YEAH?

I'M SORRY I SHOT YOU IN THE HEAD SO MANY TIMES.
NO PROBLEM.
SORRY FOR PUNCHING YOU.

WHAT KIND OF SOUP IS THIS?

IT'S GUMBO.

GUMBO?

IT'S CHICKEN AND VEGETABLE STEW.

YES! FINALLY!!

CALORIES!!

...

HERE, OKUMURA.

THIS WAS CAUGHT ON KURO'S COLLAR.

BABMP
OH! THESE WERE IN MY WAIST POUCH THE WHOLE TIME!
BABMP
OKUMURA...
...IS THIS ENOUGH STEW?
BABMP
I'LL HEAT THEM UP.
EXCELLENT!!
BABMP
NO, GIMME MORE.
BABMP

HOW ABOUT YOU, MR. OKUMURA?
!!
UH, WHAT?!

HOW MUCH DO YOU WANT?
BA BMP
UM...
...JUST A MODERATE HELPING.

HERE, OKUMURA.
OOH! IT SMELLS SPACY!
AND IT LOOKS GOOD!
SNIFF
SNIFF SNIFF
I THINK YOU MEAN *SPICY*.

HERE, MR. OKUMURA.
...

UM, SUGURO?!
ABOUT WHAT HAPPENED IN KYOTO DURING NEW YEAR'S, I'M REALLY–
HEY, YOU KNOW WHAT?
SOME-TIMES...
...CALLING ONE OF YOU OKUMURA...
...AND THE OTHER MR. OKUMURA...
?!
...CAN GET KIND OF CONFUSING.
I KNOW WHAT YOU MEAN!
SO FROM NOW ON...
...IT'S JUST RIN...
...AND YUKIO!
IS THAT FINE WITH YOU TWO?

HUH?
HUUUUH?
HA HA HA!
THAT'S... HEH HEH HEH...
OF COURSE YOU CAN!!
SO, HERE YOU GO...
...YUKIO.
YEAH, OKAY...
...THANK YOU.

I CAN'T WAIT ANY LONGER! LET'S DIG IN!!
YAAAY
LET'S EAT!
ALL RIGHT.
WOW...
...THIS IS GOOD.
IT'S DELICIOUS!
I LIKE IT!

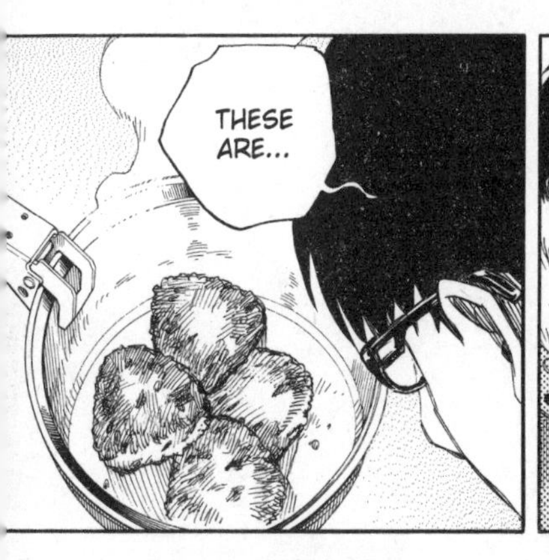

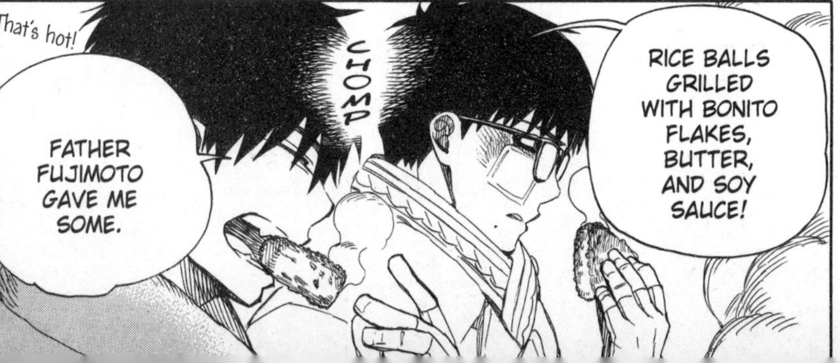

SUGURO IS EASY TO SAY, SO I'LL KEEP CALLING YOU THAT.
OKAY, FINE BY ME.
NO FAIR! I WANNA BE BUDDY-BUDDY TOO!
YOU'RE LUCKY TO EVEN BE HANGING OUT WITH US!
YOU'VE GOT SOME NERVE!
ALWAYS LEAVING IN HELICOP-TERS!
AWW, IZUMO...
...DIDJA MISS ME?
WHAT ?!
OOPS. GUESS NOT.
CHOMP
IT FEELS GOOD TO BE BACK TOGETHER.

MNCH
MNCH
THIS SURE BRINGS BACK MEMORIES!
YEAH, IT DOES...

WA HA HA HA
WHAT AN ADORABLE GUY!
You're crying!
KNOCK IT OFF.
GO EASY ON HIM, RIN...
ANYWAY, HOW'S SHIEMI?
JOLT
WELL...
...SHE'S, UM...
?!
DID SOMETHING HAPPEN?
UM...
Er...
What happened?
SOMETHING *DID* HAPPEN?!
CHATTER
Okay!
CHATTER
Be ready to fight, just in case.
CHATTER

Arrrngh!
WHAM
MAKE WAY FOR THE ARCH KNIGHT!!
BAM
RAAARGH!
BAM
THERE'S SOMEONE INSIDE THE STORAGE UNIT!!
BAM
Grarrrgh!
BAM
AAARGH!
KREAK
Nngh!
WHAM
GAAH!
I SUSPECT IT'S A REPLICANT FROM THE LABORATORY IN ROMANIA.
WHAT'S IN THERE?
WHAM
HUH? THAT SOUNDS BAD...
BAM
URRRRNGH!
BAM
URNNNNGH!!
BAM
WHAM
GCHNK
!!

RATTLE
WHAM
KRII

FUJIMOTO ?!
THERE'S NO DOUBT ABOUT IT.
IT'S A VESSEL FOR POSSESSION BY SATAN!
FALL BACK!!
MURMUR
?!
WHAT ...
...DID HE JUST SAY?!

WHAT ARE YOU WAITING FOR?!
GET BACK!
FATHER... ...FUJIMOTO?

THADOOM
BWA HA HA...
HEE HEE HEE...

Blue Exorcist Chapter 128: Of One Cloth–Shine

Chapter 129:
Of One Cloth—Felicitations

YUKIO!
GAAGH!
BAMP
!
YOUR FLAME IS–
HUFF
...
IS HE BACK?
IS SATAN BACK?!
...!
HUFF
UNGH...
HEE HEE HEE!
HA HA HA!
HEE HEE!
I FOUND YOUUUUU!
HYA HA HA HA HA!
???
WHAT HAPPENED?!

STAY BACK!
IT'S NO USE!
!!
CHATTER CHATTER
WHAT'S...
...GOING ON OVER THERE?
IT'S YUKIO...
GASP
IS HE REACTING TO THE SUBJECT?!!
?!
KEEP YUKIO OKUMURA AWAY FROM THE VESSEL OF POSSESSION!!
IT'S MERELY A DOLL WITHOUT THE ELIXIR, BUT SATAN MUST REALLY LIKE THIS FORM.
SO WE HAVE TO KILL IT!

AND EVACUATE THE AREA!

HUP HUP HUP

UNDER-STOOD.

I'LL GET THE BOY CLEAR!

IS THERE NO OTHER CHOICE?

SHUF

I'LL KILL THE VESSEL.

OSCEOLA, BE READY FOR INTERFERENCE FROM SATAN.

HWOO

LEWIN!

VREEE

HE MAY LOOK LIKE A FRIEND...

...BUT YOU CAN'T HESITATE.

LISTEN UP!!

CLEAR THE IMMEDIATE AREA AND BE READY FOR COMBAT!

HUBBUB

Get going!!
Wake up anyone still asleep!
!!
BUT...
NO!!
I DON'T HAVE TIME TO WORRY ABOUT YOU BRATS.
PICK UP YOUR BROTHER AND FOLLOW ME.
BUT *YOU* CAN STAY!
!
SERIOUSLY, LADY?!
YUP!!

HANG IN THERE, YUKIO.
HUFF
HUFF
SEE YA LATER!!
BE CAREFUL, YOU TWO!

I MUST NOT...
...!!
HUFF
Ungh...
...LOOK AT THAT.

...THEN IT WILL HAPPEN.
UNGH!
GAH!
KYAH!
MY EYES!
I CAN'T BELIEVE IT!
WAS HE ABOVE US THE WHOLE TIME?!

!!
LUCIFER!
DAMN!
HERE HE COMES!
KYA...
KYA HA...
AH HA...
KYA HA! KYA HA HA!
HEH...
... HEH ...
HEH HEH...
KYA HA!
HEE HEE...
... HEE!

KYA HA!
AH HA HA!
VDAIIIII
UGH!
BLAM
LEWIN!!
BA BA BA BA BA BA
BA BA BA BAM

KYA HA!
KYA HA!
AH HA!
BABAM
BAM BAM BAM BAM
?
OH...
LEND ME STRENGTH, OLD MAN!
BAM
BAM
BAM
BAM
"PRIMORDIAL ONE, THE FOUNDATION IS ASIZ AND THE ELEMENTS ARE HUMANKIND AND POISON.
IF THE ELEMENTS ARE DISOBEDIENT..."
UMPH
"...THEN COMMAND MY ELEMENT..."
"...AND GIVE BIRTH TO THE TRUE SKY!"
"BE STRONG!"
...
!
SWIP
?

"AND WITH STRENGTH...
...UPON STRENGTH..."
NGH!
GAK!
?!
GWO
"...CRUSH UNTO DEATH!!!!"
GRNNCH
HUFF
HUFF
"REDUCE TO NAUGHT!"
!
A SERAPHIM!
BAM BAM
BAM
OH NO!!
WHSH

KOFF

WHUPPA WHUPPA
OSCE...
...OLA...
...
D...
DOES THAT MEAN...
...IT'S... COMPLETE?
GRRR
UNK
RMMM
GRANNY!!
哎呀
WHAM
!!
RMMMM

GWGOOOOOOOM
TEE...
...HEE...
...HEE...
...HEE...
YUKIO!
RMMM
DID YOU REALLY THINK...
...THAT RATS LIKE YOU COULD STEAL WHAT BELONGS TO FATHER?
WHO'RE YOU?!
KTINK
Urgh...
GIVE BACK YUKIO!!!
BOOF
SHNK
AGH!

SO YOU'RE OUR YOUNGEST SIBLING, HUH?
HMF!
YOU'RE SURPRISINGLY CUTE.
BUT NOT AS CUTE AS EGYN.
WHAT'RE YOU TALKING ABOUT?!
DASH
I HATE TO MISS OUT, BUT...
...I'LL LET YOU *MUSPELLS* PLAY WITH HIM!
GWOOO
DOOM
WHOA!
THEY'RE HOT!
YOW!
ARGH!
MY FLAME IS STILL WEAK!
RRRRR

RMMM
YUKIO !!
RMM
RMM
RMM

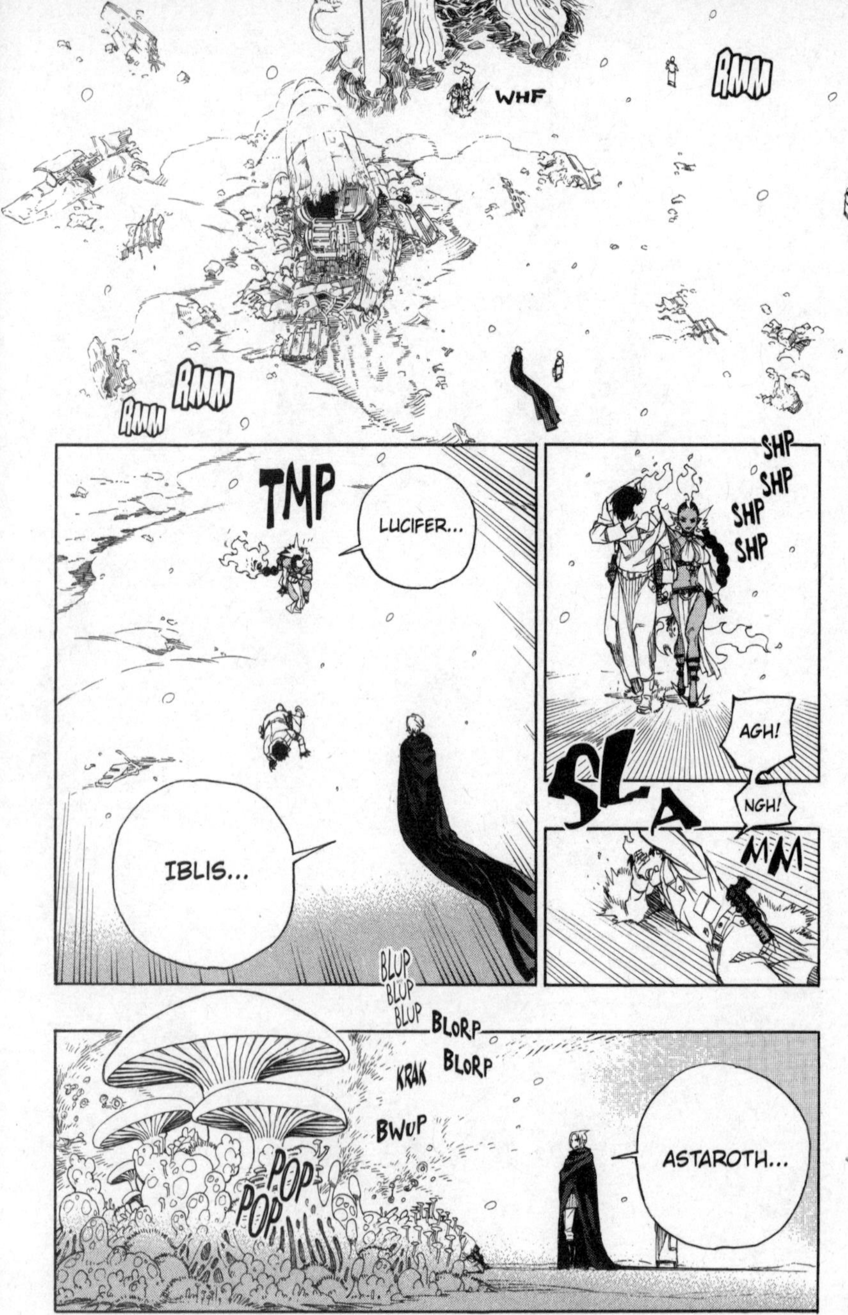
WHF
RMM
RMM
RMM
SHP
SHP
SHP
SHP
AGH!
NGH!
SLAMM
TMP
LUCIFER...
IBLIS...
BLUP
BLUP
BLUP
BLORP
BLORP
KRAK
BWUP
POP
POP
ASTAROTH...

GLUP
GLUP
LUCIFER...
GLUP
GLUP
GLUP
GLUP
EGYN...
PLOSH
GLORSH

...I SEE YOU MADE IT.
YEAH, BUT...
...UM...
...ABOUT THE, UH...
... ELIXIR ...

YOU FAILED.

W...
WELL, UM...
UM...
S-S...
...S...
...SORRY, BUT...

...I WAS ONLY ABLE TO SAVE...
...ONE DROP.
...
UH...
UM...
...LUCIFER?

I HAVE WON.
KOFF
KOFF
KOFF
COMMANDER!
I'M FINE...
...BUT SECURE THE ELIXIR!
YES, SIR!
...
BIP BIP BIP
PSHOO
K-TNK

PLIP
I HAVE IT.
KTNK
BIP
BEEP
SHOONK
?
LUCIFER?
UH, WHY...
KOFF KOFF
CLOTHES. ON THE DOUBLE!
RIGHT AWAY, SIR!
NO...
HUFF
HUFF
HUFF

THE ELIXIR IS COMPLETE?
HUFF
HUFF
HUFF
STAY CALM. AND DON'T LOOK.
DON'T UNCOVER YOUR EYE NO MATTER WHAT...
YUKIO!!
MOVE ASIDE.
GRANNY?!
NO, YOU MUST LOOK!
AND YOU KNOW THAT!
WE CAN'T JUST STAND HERE!
WE MUST RESIST WITH EVERY OUNCE OF STRENGTH!!
THAT'S RIGHT!
WE'LL FIGHT!!

IF YOU DON'T LOOK AT ME...
...THEN I WILL START KILLING AGAIN ALL OVER THE WORLD.
HHHEEEEEEE!
AND SO MANY WILL DIE!
EXACTLY AS ON THE BLUE NIGHT!
HEE HEE HEE! HAHAHAHA!
OH, RIGHT...

...THE FATEFUL DAY HAS COME!

I SEEK TO BE IN THE PRESENCE...

...OF THE FULL POWER AND GLORY...

...OF THE LORD AND SUPREME DEITY OF ALL CREATION.

...THIS WAS...
HEE!
HEH HEH!
HEH!
NOW...
...THE ONLY ANSWER!
...LOOK AT ME.

BOOOM
YUKIO !!!!
KLNK
KLNK

BOOF
BWFF
BOOF
AHH...

...THIS FEELS AMAZING!

WELL DONE, LUCIFER.
YOU HAVE COME IN *FIRST*.
IT IS AN HONOR, M'LORD.
FMP

DESTROY ASSIAH...
HUFF
...AND CREATE A WORLD WHERE DEMONS THRIVE LIKE HUMAN BEINGS.
KOFF
LUCIFER...
HUFF
HUFF
KOFF

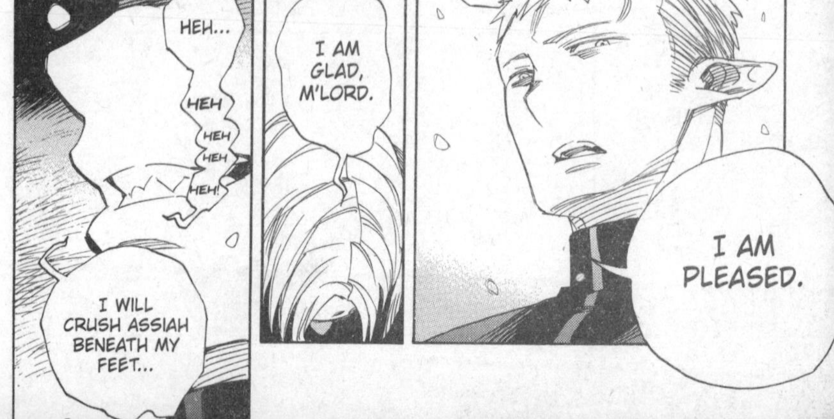

HWOOO
...AND REMAKE IT WITH THESE HANDS!
KRAKL
...I SHALL DO ALL ACCORDING TO MY WILL!
HEE HEE!
WITH THESE HANDS...
HWOOOOO
GWO
BLUP BLUP BLUP
KRIK KRIK
RUSTLE
RUSTLE
KOFF
KOFF
?!
BWOP
PWUP
PWUP
WHAT THE...
BWOP
KYAAAH!
GYAIEEE
GYEEEE
GYAAAAH
GYAH
CALM DOWN!!
SKIT-TER-SKIT-TER
YES, I AM MOST PLEASED!!
W-WHAT'S GOING ON?!
S...
SOMETHING IS HAPPENING!!
RUSTLE
RUSTLE
RUSTLE

GO FORTH AND CRUSH THEM!

Blue Exorcist Chapter 129: Of One Cloth—Felicitations

Chapter 130: Of One Cloth—Gleam

ONE WEEK IN HERE...

...IS TEN MINUTES OUT THERE.

NOW I WILL INTRODUCE YOUR FINAL CHALLENGE.

!!

THIS TREE IS A CRYSTALLIZATION OF SHEMIHAZA...
...RIGHT?
YES.
I MUST TELL YOU WHY SHEMIHAZA CRYSTALLIZED LIKE THIS.
TAK
TAK
TAK

LONG AGO...
...THE LAND WAS MADE BARREN AND INHOSPITABLE TO LIFE BY THE KING OF EARTH.
TO QUELL HIS ANGER...
...SHEMIHAZA SACRIFICED HER FLESH AND CRYSTALLIZED.
THE KING OF EARTH?
LOOK THERE.
DO YOU SEE THE LARGE MINERALS AMONG THE CRYSTAL'S ROOTS?

THOSE ARE THE SEALED CRYSTALLIZATIONS OF AMAIMON, KING OF EARTH.
?!
BUT...
...DOESN'T AMAIMON HAVE A HUMAN BODY?!
He pretends to be a student at True Cross Academy.
THAT...
...IS MERELY PART OF AMAIMON.
SHEMIHAZA TOOK PITY ON THE KING OF EARTH...
...SO SHE LEFT HIM HIS "SELF" IN EXCHANGE FOR HIM BECOMING HER SERVANT.
S...
SO THEN...
TMP
TMP TMP TMP TMP

THOOOM
AS YOUR FINAL CHALLENGE...
WAAAH!
...YOU MUST SUBJUGATE THE KING OF EARTH.
VMM
VMM
VMM
VMM

...!!
YOU HAVE THE BASIC ABILITIES.
WHAT YOU LACK IS CONFIDENCE..
...WHICH YOU WILL GAIN...
...IF YOU CAN OVERCOME THIS CHALLENGE.
SWOO

FAREWELL, SHIEMI.
I CAN GUIDE YOU NO FURTHER.
GRANDMA!
I PASSED AWAY SUDDENLY, SO...
...I HAVE ENJOYED THE LAST YEAR AND A HALF WITH YOU...
...AS YOUR GUARDIAN SPIRIT.
ME TOO...
ME TOO!!

SHIEMI...
...I'M SURE YOU'LL BE OKAY.
GRANDMA ...
...THANK YOU.
AH, WELL...
I KNEW IT...

SO YOU'RE THE *SUCCESSOR*, HUH?

COULDA FOOLED *ME*.

PTOO

ARE YOU SURE ABOUT THAT?

YOU SHOULD BE SCARED OF ME.

I CAN'T LOSE.

OH. TOUGH TALK, HUH?
...
BWOOM
THEN BRING IT ON!
THIS TIME...

...I'M GONNA HELP EVERY-ONE!!

BLAM
HUFF
BLAM
HUFF
HUFF
BLAM
GASP
GYAAAH!
HELP ME!!
GO TO HIGH GROUND...
...AND ADMINISTER THE ELIXIR TO THE COMMANDER.
Y...
YES, SIR!!
KOFF
I LEAVE THE REST TO YOU...
...HOMARE.
UNDER-STOOD.
KREE
KREE
RIP
SNAP
POP
SHF
SHF
SHF
TH...
THIS IS...
HA...
HA HA! HEE HEE HEE!
AT LAST...
FINALLY!!!
LOOK!

WHAT A BEAUTIFUL SIGHT!
RMM
OUR BROTHER ASTAROTH IS OVERJOYED!
THEY'RE ALL LIVING IT UP!
RMM
RMM

THAT'S RIGHT, DARLING EGYN. ♡
IT TRULY IS AN ACT OF GOD.
OUR ARDENT DESIRE IS FINALLY BECOMING REAL!
RMM

HMM...
VMM
YES, THAT'S IT...
VMM
VMM
I MUST WHITTLE DOWN THE HUMANS...
VMM
...AND I'LL START BY KILLING THE EXORCISTS!

KRA
WAAH!!
KOOM
THRUM THRUM
THRUM THRUM
THE DEFENSIVE MAGIC WALL ISN'T STRONG ENOUGH!!
THERE AREN'T ENOUGH ARIAS! HELP US!
WHAT HAPPENED TO RIN AND YUKIO?
ARE THEY OKAY?!
WE'RE IN DANGER TOO, YA KNOW!!
LIGHTNING!!
HA HA HA HA HA!
THINK YOU CAN RESIST, EH?

WELL, HOW DO YOU LIKE THIS?
SWP
HWOOO
RMM
RMM
RMM
IT'S HUGE!
PROTECT THE ARIAS AT ALL COSTS!!
RMM

YOU MAGGOTS!
...
?!
HUH?
CHATTER
WHAT HAPPENED?
CHATTER
THE LIGHTNING STOPPED IN MIDAIR!

?!
SPACE HAS WARPED !!
GLORP
SORRY TO KEEP YOU WAITING...
POOF
...ALL YOU MEPHISTO FANS OUT THERE! ♡
?!
TIK
TIK
TIK
TIK
WASN'T IT ABOUT TIME I SHOWED UP? ☆

!!
WE'RE SAVED!!
SIR PHELES!
YOU HAVE FIVE MINUTES AT MOST...
...SO YOU BETTER REGROUP!
LIGHTNING ?!!
AS YOU CAN SEE, ALL HELL IS BREAKING LOOSE HERE!
RIN!
YUKIO!
ARE YOU ALL RIGHT?!
HEY, EVERY-ONE!
OSCEOLA'S WOUNDED OVER HALF HIS BODY.
YES, SIR!
TAKE YUKIO TOO!
TAKE HIM TO THE VATICAN.
HE'S INJURED.

OH NO! YUKIO'S BLEEDING!
I'M OKAY.
IT'S JUST A CUT FROM MY GLASSES BREAKING.
THEN YOU NEED FIRST AID!
NO...
...I HAVE TO SAY SOMETHING FIRST.
Thank you.
LIGHTNING...
...IT'S MY FAULT THAT SATAN RETURNED.

I *CHOSE* TO LOOK.

SO I APOLOGIZE.

MM...

SO LET'S TAKE HIM DOWN!
AS LONG AS DEMONS THREATEN US...
...WE HAVE NO OTHER CHOICE.

PAT
ISN'T THAT RIGHT?!
YES, THAT'S RIGHT.
YOU'RE A TEACHER, SO NO WONDER YOU'RE SMART!!
OKAY, OKAY...
DEFEATING SATAN WILL WARP THE WORLD, SO I WAS TRYING TO AVOID IT...
...BUT I GUESS THAT'S HOW IT'S GOTTA GO.
LET'S GET THIS PARTY STARTED, SIR PHELES.
?!

FLIK

INITIATE PLAN B!

PAPAPOOF

I'VE GATHERED EXORCISTS AND VOLUNTEER DEMONS FROM ACROSS THE GLOBE...

KCHAK KCHAK KCHAK

...TO FORM THE ANTI-SATAN SUPPRESSION FORCE!

THESE MEMBERS OF WELL-KNOWN FAMILIES, LONERS, OUTCASTS, AND OTHER ORGANIZATIONS ...
...ARE A TOTAL MISH-MASH...
...BUT THEY'RE ALSO FAMOUS *EXORCISTS*!!
DA DUM
FWEEET
DUM
CLANG
DUM
KLANG
HUH ?!
IS THAT THE KING OF INSECTS??!
YIKES! BUGS?!
CHATTER
WHOA!!

AND THERE'S SHEMIHAZA!
WHOA
IS THE GRIGORI GUARD...
...GOING TO FIGHT ?!
SHEMI-HAZA...
ONE OF THE GRIGORI...
SO?
WHAT A RELIEF, YEAH?
PAT
ANYWAY, STOP WORRYING ABOUT EVERYTHING.
?!

I WAS...

...HA HA... HA...

...TAKING EVERY-THING UPON MYSELF AGAIN...

UM, OKAY...

...JUST LIKE A CHILD.

HA HA HA! FINALLY SOMETHING EVEN *I* CAN UNDERSTAND!

IN OTHER WORDS...
KRAKL
KRAKL
...IT'S TIME TO KICK SATAN'S ASS!!
FOOOM
RIGHT?!

AM I RIGHT, YUKIO?

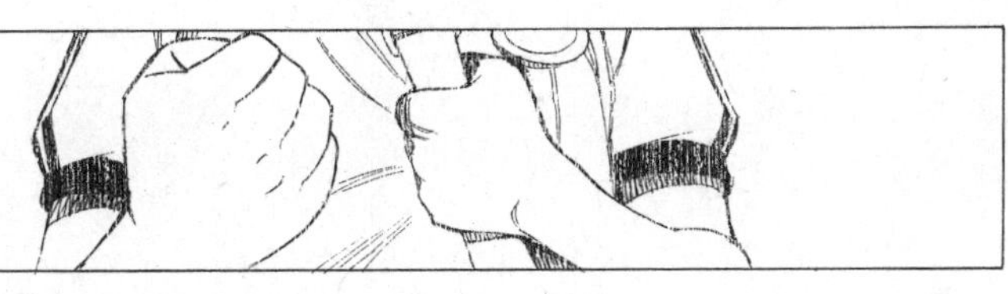

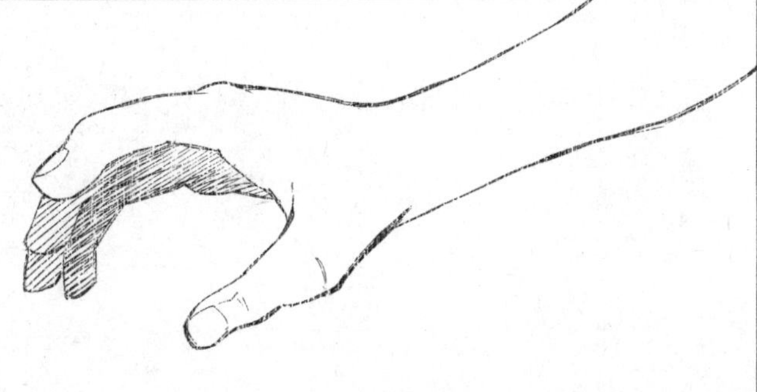

YEAH...

LET'S KICK HIS ASS.

HEY, I WANT IN ON THIS TOO!
AWESOME !!
GLOMP
I WANNA KICK HIS BUTT TOO. If it looks doable...
BAM
YEAH!
SEEMS LIKE WE HAVE A MOTTO...
LET'S KICK SATAN'S BUTT!!
IF IT LOOKS DOABLE, I'M ALL FOR IT!
GYA HA HA HA WA HA HA
THE KIDS ARE GETTING GOOFY...
WELL, THAT'S A LOT BETTER THAN GLOOMY.

WE CAN ALL...
...GO KICK SATAN'S BUTT TOGETHER!

BLUE EXORCIST 27 - END -

Blue Exorcist Chapter 130: Of One Cloth—Gleam

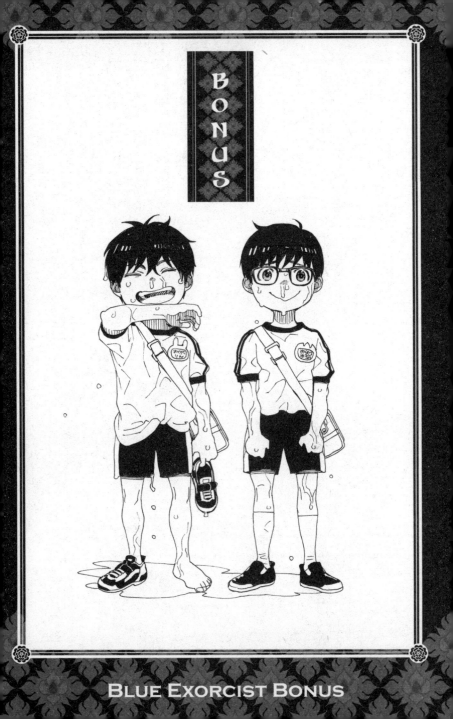

Blue Exorcist Bonus

WHEN I GET OUTTA THIS JOINT...
...I'M GONNA DEDICATE MYSELF TO OTHERS.

OH? LIKE HOW?

I'LL INCLUDE A Q&A ...
...AND DEMON GUIDE ENTRIES ...
...AND CHARACTER PROFILES...

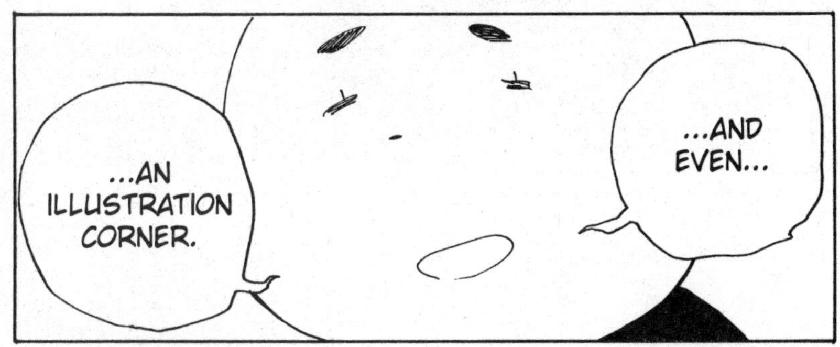
...AND EVEN...
...AN ILLUSTRATION CORNER.

AN ILLUSTRATION CORNER?
CRIME AND PUNISHMENT
CHIPS
IS THAT EVEN POSSIBLE?

BLUE EXORCIST

AOEX! 27!!!

Art Staff

HOW ABOUT A NENDOROID?
I MADE THE PURCHASE!
A BLIND SPOT!
MY STOMACH...

Erika Uemura

Ryoji Hayashi

Mari Oda

Aki Shiina

Art Assistants

I CAN'T FORGET GORO.
IS THAT ALL RIGHT?!
I'VE NEVER WATCHED FURUHATA NINZABURO.
I'M WATCHING A KIRIN VIDEO.

Yamanaka-san

Obata-san

Ito-kun

Seo-san

Composition Assistant

Minoru Sasaki

Research Cooperation

Daisuke Hunt Okumiya-san

I'LL DO IT!!

Ryosuke Honda-san
(MMA Rangers Gym)

Editor

I ROLLED GACHA IN UMAMUSUME!

Ippei Sawada

Graphic Novel Editor

IT'S UNKNOWN TERRITORY...

Ryusuke Kuroki

Graphic Novel Design

THANKS FOR THE GREAT WORK!!

Shimada Hideaki

Rie Akutsu (L.S.D.)

Manga

YOUTUBE IS GETTING ENGROSSING!

Kazue Kato

(In no particular order)
(Note: The caricatures and statements are from memory!)

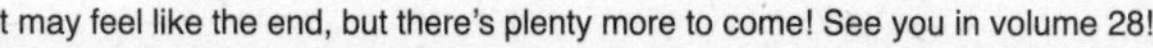
It may feel like the end, but there's plenty more to come! See you in volume 28!!

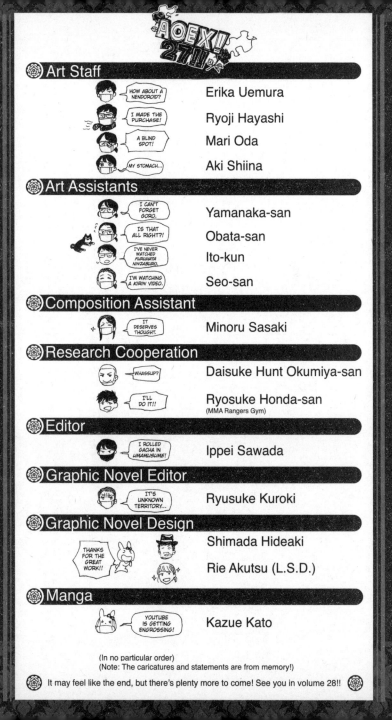

You can guess the situation, right?
Yep... that's it! Guilty as charged!!

The reconciled brothers perform a stunt!
HUP HUP
Gya ha ha ha!
Whoa ...

Kazue Kato

In volume 26 I said I wanted to eat some barbecue. My cousin in Hokkaido sent me some meat. It was really delicious! I'm very thankful.

I'm deeply moved that I've been able to get this far with the series.

I hope you enjoyed volume 27.

BLUE EXORCIST

BLUE EXORCIST VOL. 27
SHONEN JUMP Edition

STORY & ART BY KAZUE KATO

Translation & English Adaptation/John Werry
Touch-Up Art & Lettering/John Hunt, Primary Graphix
Cover & Interior Design/Julian [JR] Robinson
Editor/Mike Montesa

Printed in the U.S.A.

Published by VIZ Media, LLC
P.O. Box 77010
San Francisco, CA 94107

10 9 8 7 6 5 4 3 2 1
First printing, May 2022

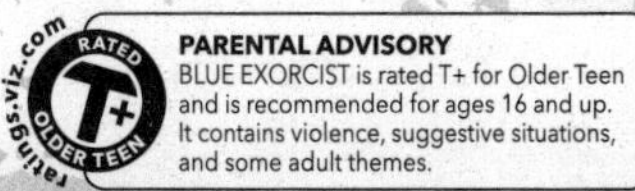

In the next volume...

Shiemi confronts her old nemesis Amaimon. The demon king of earth doesn't understand just how powerful Shiemi has become, but for Shiemi to achieve her destiny, she also needs to realize her own strength! Back in Assiah, Satan and his minions square off against Mephisto and the Knights of the True Cross to determine the fate of the world. After receiving some enchanted power-ups, the Exwires prepare to enact their battle plan. Rin himself is part of the vanguard that aims to engage the enemy head-on. The time has come for Rin to fulfill his promise to defeat the King of Demons, Satan!

Coming soon!

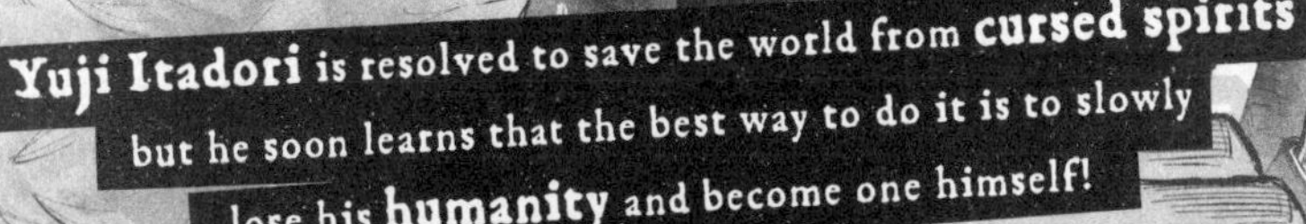
Yuji Itadori is resolved to save the world from **cursed spirits**
but he soon learns that the best way to do it is to slowly
lose his **humanity** and become one himself!

JUJUTSU KAISEN

STORY AND ART BY
GEGE AKUTAMI

In a world where **cursed spirits** feed on unsuspecting humans, fragments of the legendary and feared demon **Ryomen Sukuna** were lost and scattered about. Should any demon consume Sukuna's body parts, the power they gain could **destroy the world** as we know it. Fortunately, there exists a mysterious school of **Jujutsu Sorcerers** who exist to protect the precarious existence of the living from the **supernatural**!

RATED
T+
OLDER TEEN
VIZ

You're Reading in the Wrong Direction!!

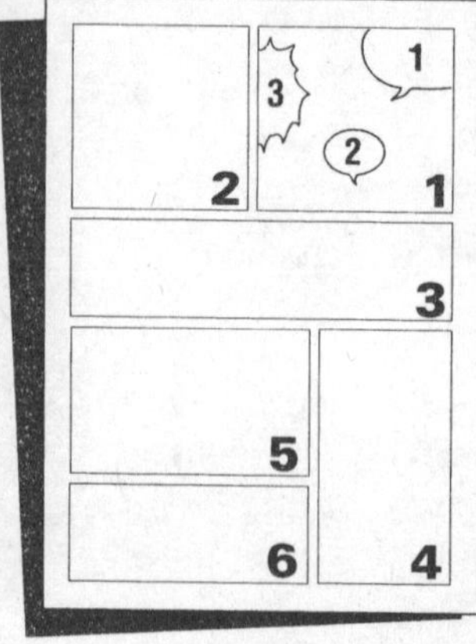

Whoops! Guess what? You're starting at the wrong end of the comic!

...It's true! In keeping with the original Japanese format, **Blue Exorcist** is meant to be read from right to left, starting in the upper-right corner.

Unlike English, which is read from left to right, Japanese is read from right to left, meaning that action, sound effects, and word-balloon order are completely reversed... something which can make readers unfamiliar with Japanese feel pretty backwards themselves. For this reason, manga or Japanese comics published in the U.S. in English have sometimes been published "flopped"—that is, printed in exact reverse order, as though seen from the other side of a mirror.

By flopping pages, U.S. publishers can avoid confusing readers, but the compromise is not without its downside. For one thing, a character in a flopped manga series who once wore in the original Japanese version a T-shirt emblazoned with "M A Y" (as in "the merry month of") now wears one which reads "Y A M"! Additionally, many manga creators in Japan are themselves unhappy with the process, as some feel the mirror-imaging of their art skews their original intentions.

We are proud to bring you Kazue Kato's **Blue Exorcist** in the original unflopped format. For now, though, turn to the other side of the book and let the adventure begin...!

—Editor